Rites for a New Age

Understanding the
Book of Alternative Services

Michael Ingham

The Anglican Book Centre
Toronto, Ontario

1986
Anglican Book Centre
600 Jarvis Street
Toronto, Ontario
Canada M4Y 2J6

Typesetting by Jay Tee Graphics
Printed and bound in Canada

Canadian Cataloguing in Publication Data

Ingham, Michael
  Rites for a new age: understanding the Book of alternative
  services

ISBN 0-919891-52-7

1.Anglican Church of Canada.   The book of alternative services of the
Anglican Church of Canada.   I. Title.

BX5616.153 1986   264'.03   C86-094396-8

Contents

For Gwen,
intuitive liturgist

Preface to the First Edition

Liturgical change evokes quite contrary reactions in people. For some, it is a cause for excitement and renewed interest in the church. For others, it is a source of dismay and unease, as if the church had voluntarily cut its own anchor and set itself adrift. This book arises from the struggles and searchings around the new and old services of a small congregation of faithful Christians on the West Coast. It was begun in the hope of discovering some reasons for liturgical change which has, in our place as in many others, produced some consternation and perplexity. In particular, it is an effort to move beyond the rather arid and fruitless discussions about differences of style and wording between the Prayer Book and the *Book of Alternative Services* to the more interesting questions of the differences in content and substance.

What do the old and new rites have to say about the world in which we live, for instance? What do they say about ministry in the world, about spirituality, about community, about mission and evangelism, about sexuality? They don't always say the same things. My argument in these pages is that the context of the church has changed profoundly since the days when the Prayer Book was written, that we have entered a period of post-Christendom, and that the new rites of the church are intended to equip us for ministry and mission in a new age. If the book succeeds in focusing some attention away from debates about "change for the sake of change" to the importance of the relationship between liturgy and Christian life, I shall be well pleased.

Perhaps it might help you the reader to know that in our parish we have two principal Sunday services. One uses the traditional rite, the other the contemporary. There is no unanimity among us about which is the better. Most of us are comfortable with both, and see the value of both, but some are committed exclusively to one or to the other and attend celebrations of the "wrong" liturgy only with great reluctance. Even so, to them I am extremely indebted. Their probings and questionings have challenged me to delve much more deeply into liturgy than ever I did in seminary. Those who have objected to liturgical change, especially those who have done so in love, have enriched my understanding of worship greatly, and though we may not in the end agree, I believe we have learned much from each other. However, to those whose willingness has made it possible to explore the depths and breadths of the new rites, and to mine their spiritual gold with some enthusiasm and joy, I would like to say how much of a privilege it has been and continues to be.

I should like to mention that, in the interests of verbal economy, this book refers frequently to "the Prayer Book" as if there has been only one. There have been, of course, many versions of the Prayer Book since the first edition of 1549, but the one most familiar to contemporary Anglicans is the 1959/1962 version and wherever possible I have confined my illustrations and examples to this. Occasionally, the point I wish to make is more clearly demonstrated from the 1662 version, or from the English Missal, in which case the date and the book is indicated. Properly speaking, of course, it is better to think of a Prayer Book tradition, rather than any particular version of it. It is that tradition which has now come to its conclusion with the *Book of Alternative Services.* The words "Prayer Book" should therefore be taken to mean that family of rites which forms a continuous tradition from 1549 to 1962. It's just that it's cumbersome to say that every time.

I should like to thank a wonderful group of adventuresome Anglicans who gathered at Sorrento Centre in British Columbia in the summer of 1985, and who were the first to experience these musings. Their suggestions and criticisms have been invaluable. Especially, I must thank Mona Morley who took such excellent notes that I was able later to reconstruct what I actually said, and to review much of it.

And my warmest thanks to my wife Gwen, who tells me every Sunday how the liturgy is being experienced in the community I serve. It really is a gift of grace to have at one's side the friendliest and most perceptive of observers.

Michael Ingham
St. Francis-in-the-Wood
West Vancouver, B.C.

Preface to the Third Printing

The publication of this third printing of *Rites For A New Age* gives me an opportunity to reflect on the state of the church's worship five years after the appearance of *The Book of Alternative Services*, and to respond to some of the comments that have been made about my book.

When the first printing of *Rites* appeared in 1986 it was too early to predict how *The Book of Alternative Services* would be received in our church. *Rites* was written shortly after the *BAS* came off the press, and it was intended to be a study of the thematic content of the new rites, not a "how to" book about introducing the *BAS* into a parish. It was, and is, offered as a resource to people exploring the reasons for liturgical change as a ground for understanding the meaning of worship and its relation to the modern world.

The actual process of liturgical change is an important matter, however, and requires more than a study such as this. Coping with change is not a purely rational endeavour for any of us. There are a number of people who have a genuinely visceral reaction to it, whom no amount of rational explanation will impress. As Pascal remarked, "the heart has its reasons of which reason knows not." Still, I confess I have been surprised and dismayed at the insensitivity with which *The Book of Alternative Services* has been introduced in some places, and at the failure to adapt to the opportunities for dignified and coherent celebration which the liturgies afford. There is still a tendency simply to replace the old book with the new and then to use the new rites in the old way, without discerning the internal logic of the new liturgies and the implications for liturgical movement, music, and physical architecture. Someone needs to write another book about all that. I have been equally astonished at the condescension and vehemence with which *The Book of Alternative Services* has been opposed by some traditionalist campaigners claiming to speak for the majority of Anglicans.

Looking back on the last five years and on the words I wrote then, I would have to say that I have changed my mind on at least one assumption which appears fairly prominently in this book.

When *Rites For A New Age* first appeared I assumed we were heading into a future of two distinct but compatible liturgical traditions. I envisioned a future in which most Anglicans would have ready access to both the *BAS* and the *BCP*. I still believe that to be an acceptable and desirable situation. The reality, however, is proving to be different. We are steadily becoming a church of two separate liturgical camps. I have received numerous letters from people complaining they cannot find one or other liturgical tradition in their own church, and have to move around from parish to parish in order to experience either traditional or contemporary worship. This might be an inexorable historical development. On the other hand, it looks to me like liturgical ghettoism.

The Book of Alternative Services has clearly become the dominant tradition. Its introduction has been widely accepted in most parts of Canada and in many churches it is used exclusively at the principal liturgy on Sundays. For the most part this development seems to have been accomplished easily and without disruption. In Western Canada the process appears to be furthest developed, while the picture becomes more of a patchwork as one moves east, with some very traditional centres in Toronto and the Maritime provinces maintaining their commitment to the older liturgies. In some places you find a church of one persuasion clearly isolated in a surrounding ocean of the other. But the overall pattern is clear. The *BAS* has commended itself to the church, and it has done so for a variety of reasons and in a multiplicity of ways, with the result that it is becoming the normative form of worship for Anglicans in this country. While the *Book of Common Prayer* has not disappeared, it is no longer in use in large parts of the country. This trend is more apparent now than it was five years ago and there is no indication that it will be reversed.

The pattern is likely to continue as clergy trained largely in the contemporary tradition move into positions of parish leadership, and as new generations of members — for whom the *BAS* is the only known form of Anglican worship — grow up in the church.

While the *Book of Common Prayer* is likely to retain its place of honour within Anglicanism, it will probably do so less as a living form of worship in all but a few churches. Those who find this prospect profoundly sad will no doubt keep the Prayer Book alive in their own place of worship. Those who do not will probably look upon the *BCP* as a familiar friend which has gone the way of other familiar friends into the mists of time and fond memory.

Since the appearance of *The Book of Alternative Services* in 1985 we have witnessed two events unique in our history. One is the convening of the Supreme Court of Appeal to hear arguments for and against the validity of ordinations and consecrations conducted according to the new rites. The second is the formation of the Prayer Book Society of Canada, an organisation whose purpose is to uphold the *Book of Common Prayer* as normative for Anglicanism. Both these events have changed the climate of debate and discussion in our church. The first has moved us into a litigious age, in which law is seen to be the ground for determining gospel. The second has moved us into an age of party factionalism, in which bitter exchange and self-righteous assertion threaten to become the dominant style of theological discourse.

Perhaps litigiousness and division are inevitable developments in a church which so closely mirrors the society in which we live. But I and many others had hoped that Christians could settle their differences in a different way. It may be that legal combat in the courtroom can sometimes ferret out the truth of a difficult matter, and that adversarial argument is often an invaluable instrument for discerning justice, but it is also true that the appeal to law seldom settles a matter of conscience, and that party strife in the church has rarely done us any beneficial service.

In my view, the emergence of a Prayer Book "party" has not served the church well, nor indeed the *Book of Common Prayer*. Certainly, there has been a revival of liturgical education in some of the communities subscribing to the Society's point of view. In rejecting the *BAS*, some opponents have delved deeply into the roots of Anglican liturgical history and discovered more about the Prayer Book tradition than they knew before they started defending it. This is undoubtedly a good thing. But the emotionalism and *ad hominem* quality of some of the writing and speeches have clouded the issues and made the opponents reluctant to meet in open debate.

Nor, in my view, has the resort to the civil and ecclesiastical courts vindicated the cause of either the *Book of Common Prayer* or *The Book of Alternative Services*. It may be true that the greatness of our church has been demonstrated by the fact that a single member has had access to our highest court. But I frankly doubt that the cost to the church and its members of about $100,000 was worth the point. It seems to me that when a matter of faith and doctrine is brought before a legal body for resolution the cause is lost before it starts, whatever the outcome. Law — even canon law — is of dubious value as a tool for validating the beliefs and teachings of the church. A comment in a letter by American Anglican William Reed Huntington, writing at the turn of the century, puts this point precisely:

> [Such] a Court of Appeal is in itself inconsistent with that very genius of the Anglican Communion upon which our Catholic heritage rests. From the dawn of the Reformation in England until today, our strength has been that we have not settled doctrinal differences. By our genius for comprehensiveness we have united irreconcileables, and gloried in the simultaneous possession of doctrinal positions radically incompatible. . . . One of the foundation stones upon which we have builded, is the conviction that the best way to settle our differences is not to settle them.

Huntington's sentiment is quite traditional in Anglicanism, which has been characterised more than anything else by a spirit of tolerance and inclusivity, even doctrinal inclusivity. The great Anglican divine Richard Hooker (c. 1554-1600) appealed for an end to campaigns for ecclesiastical purity and encouraged the warring factions of his day to seek "not a compromise for the sake of peace, but . . . a comprehension for the sake of truth." Anglican comprehensiveness has been a hallmark of our theology and our worship from the beginning. Indeed, the Prayer Book tradition itself exemplifies this. Yet the events of the last five years in Canada run counter to that spirit, and point to the emergence of both legalism and purism in our post-Christendom church, a development which I find disappointing.

One word about the title of this book. To my considerable discomfort, a great deal of fuss has been made about the words "new age." In the mid-1980s, about the time of the publication of *Rites*, the New Age movement came into media prominence in some parts of North America and Europe. I'm afraid I had not even heard of it when I was doing my research. What I have been able to discover suggests that "new age spirituality" is at best an effort at scientific mysticism, an attempt to harmonise selected strands of Far Eastern religions with elements of Western post-Einstein cosmology, and at worst a Hollywood sales promotion for the careers of former screen stars. In either case, I am not an advocate for it. I am inclined to agree with the primate's observation that the relation of New Age to true religion is rather like that of Muzak to Bach. It seems to be a contemporary version of what Elijah and the prophets would have called "folk religion." My use of the words "new age" is strictly descriptive and not coded to mean something else. At any rate, no one who has read my book could imagine I have anything at all to say about "energy," channelling, or Shirley MacLaine!

Within the last five years I have moved from parish ministry, where I had spent my ordained life, into the primate's office in Toronto. The change of work has given me significant new insights into the church as a whole, and a perspective on regional issues and developments which I could never have gained otherwise. It has also meant that I have come out of the pulpit and into the pews again as a parish member. That experience has been salutary, and I am more than ever convinced that the liturgy of the church is the single most powerful and formative influence on the lives of Christians. It needs to be done well, whatever rite it is. And it needs to speak to the world in which the people of the church have to live. I believe *The Book of Alternative Services* does that, and in *Rites For A New Age* I have tried to say how it does that. This third printing is unchanged from the first because, with the exception of these few comments, I stand by what I wrote five years ago. It seems to me that time has supported the thesis this book proposes: that worship is a living tradition through which God renews the church for mission and ministry.

Michael Ingham
Toronto 1990

1. A Living Tradition

And as to the several variations from the former Book, whether by Alteration, Addition, or otherwise, it shall suffice to give this general account, That most of the Alterations were made, either first, for the better direction of them that are to officiate in any part of the Divine Service; which is chiefly done in the Calendars and Rubrics; Or secondly, for the more proper expressing of some words or phrases of ancient usage in terms more suitable to the language of the present times, and the clearer explanation of some other words and phrases, that were either of doubtful signification, or otherwise liable to misconstruction: Or thirdly, for a more perfect rendering of such portions of Holy Scripture, as are inserted into the Liturgy; which, in the Epistles and Gospels especially, and in sundry other places, are now ordered to be read according to the last Translation. . . . If any man, who shall desire a more particular account of the several Alterations in any part of the Liturgy, shall take the pains to compare the present Book with the former; we doubt not but that the reason of the change may easily appear. (from the preface to the 1662 Prayer Book)

Liturgical Change

For 400 years Anglicans have been the people of the Prayer Book. It has defined us as the Latin Mass once defined Roman Catholics. It was our badge of identity, a symbol of the unity of our worldwide communion. Wherever one travelled, one could be sure of finding the Prayer Book in one of its versions in use in any Anglican church anywhere in the world. We came to rely on its familiar presence in our pews. It provided a dependable and sure point of reference in unstable, changing times.

Now all that is changing too. Our ceremonies and rites are in a process of revision not experienced since the 16th century. In Canada, the 1980 General Synod decided that no further attempt should be made to revise the Prayer Book after its last amendment in 1959, but that a collection of alternative, contemporary rites should be compiled and published in a single book. For a while, throughout the 1970s, we had become the people of the pamphlets, as new and widely divergent liturgies were produced and distributed by in-dividual dioceses and parishes. The decision of 1980 meant that there was to be some uniformity brought into the liturgical confusion that then existed in the church. Anglicans were to be offered a book of alternative services which was to live alongside — not to replace — the Prayer Book. The hope of the General Synod was that Canadian Anglicans would have opportunity to become as familiar with the new rites as they were with the old, so that in a mobile society people would still feel bound together by a common order of worship, whether in the contemporary or in the traditional forms.

But Anglicans have never taken kindly to changes in their wor-ship. From the very beginning, the introduction of new ceremonies into the church has required long periods of painful adjustment and careful explanation. The compilers of the first *Book of Common Prayer*, which was intended to express the unique and particular identity of the Anglican church after the Reformation, had to con-tend with furious theological attacks from both Catholic and Protes-tant theologians, as well as with a general groundswell of rejection by ordinary churchpeople. With an irony characteristic of our tradi-tion ever since, Anglicans in those days demonstrated more visible concern about the new Prayer Book than they did about the takeover of the church by the state. In London a few diehards were hanged. In Cornwall a rebellion broke out among people protesting the introduction of English into church services, and the local duke was able to suppress the riots only with the help of German troops.

Liturgical change has not been accomplished easily. This is true of all Christian traditions, of course, not simply our own. We have witnessed in the last twenty years the struggle of Roman Catholics to adapt to the new directions established by the Second Vatican Coun-cil. In the developing world the post-colonial period has touched off a search for authentic and indigenous liturgy, a task remarkably similar to that undertaken by the sixteenth-century liturgical reformers. On this continent and in Europe, Presbyterians, Lutherans, Methodists, and Baptists have all begun the work of revising the forms of church services that have been in use for many hundreds of years. Throughout the Christian church today there is a ferment of activity not seen since the days when our separate liturgical traditions were formed. In all of them there is unease in some quarters, and impatience in others. After a long period of stability and predictability, we are once again facing the prospect of change, but with it we are also facing the opportunity to rediscover the power and depth of liturgy.

Liturgy as Holy Ground

Consider for a moment the power of liturgy. The scriptures contain several examples of dramatic encounters with God that take place in the context of worship. Luke's gospel, for instance, relates the meeting between Jesus and two of his followers on the road to Emmaus after the Resurrection. After journeying some way together, they stopped to eat, and during the meal they came to see that they were in the presence of the risen Christ:

> And when he sat down with them at table, he took bread and said the blessing; he broke the bread, and offered it to them. Then their eyes were opened and they recognized him. (Luke 24: 30)

This meal is the first example in the New Testament of a post-Easter celebration of the eucharist. It is the first of several occasions when the disciples met Jesus again in the breaking of bread. Through the sharing of this act they were able to enter into a real and deep communion with the risen Lord, and in the power of this communion were formed into a solid and lasting fellowship which enabled them to witness to the truth of the resurrection.

These meals, of course, were quite unlike the celebrations of the eucharist we are familiar with today. They were actual meals in which people ate and drank to satisfy their hunger and thirst. The eucharist evolved into a symbolic meal only later as the sacredness of the event became more and more evident in the experience of the early Christians. If you have ever experienced the death of a close friend you will know that the last hours you spend together are charged with a special significance that you carry for ever afterwards in your memory. Each word and gesture that passes between you is full of the recollections of happier days and better times, now tinged with a wistful poignancy and grief. When it is over, you never forget how you parted, what was said, and what was left unsaid. So it was with the disciples. After Easter, they remembered the last act they had shared with Jesus, and his instruction to them to "do this in remembrance of me."

They returned to the meal again and again. They discovered that, in sharing this common act, the risen Christ came to meet them. In a mystery which has been repeated over and over in the lives of Christians since then, the eucharistic celebration became the meeting ground between the earthly church and the risen Lord. There are many instances in the New Testament and in church history of this powerful liturgical experience, but perhaps the most striking instance in all scripture is in the Old Testament. In the Book of Isaiah we have an account of an extraordinary encounter between the prophet and Yahweh, a dramatic meeting that took place in the context of a formal public liturgy, during a service in the temple at Jerusalem. It is worth recounting, as an example of how an act of formal worship can yield an unexpected encounter with God.

The Call of Isaiah

> In the year of King Uzziah's death, I saw the Lord seated on a throne, high and exalted. (Isaiah 6:1)

The narrator sets the scene for us with brilliant clarity and brevity. It was a time of uncertainty in Judah after the death of a king. In the temple, the people had gathered for the annual celebration of one of pre-exilic Judaism's richest liturgies. The ceremony was called the Festival of the Enthronement of Yahweh. In it, a great golden throne was brought into the building with a vast procession. The throne symbolized the lordship of God, and the liturgy, which featured assembled choirs, consisted of the singing of psalms along with the reading of scriptural texts praising the majesty and holiness of God. Incense filled the sanctuary and poured down into the aisles, while the people sang and prayed and glorified God who, they hoped, would one day appear on the throne in their midst and exalt them in triumph and salvation.

In this particular year, one of the members of the congregation was the young man Isaiah. Perhaps we might speculate that the ceremony was for him, at its outset at least, just another service among the many he had attended, albeit a particularly splendid and lavish one. But during the course of it something happened that was to change Isaiah's life and the lives of the people of Judah for ever, a moment so rare that the heart almost stops to think about it. God appeared on the throne. In Isaiah's eyes, though not in those of the other people around him, the thing for which the congregation was praying happened. "I saw the Lord high and lifted up." At some indeterminate moment in the liturgy, he was suddenly confronted by the majesty of Yahweh, the empty throne was occupied, and all the elements of the Jerusalem temple became transposed into the furnishings of a heavenly court:

> The skirt of his robe filled the temple. About him were attendant seraphim, and each had six wings; one pair covered his face and one pair his feet, and one pair was spread in flight. They were calling ceaselessly to one another. "Holy, holy, holy, is the Lord of Hosts: the whole earth is full of his glory." And as each one called, the threshold shook to its foundations, while the house was filled with smoke.

The elements of this narrative move back and forth between the temple service and the simultaneous liturgy in the courts of heaven to which Isaiah had been mystically transported. The skirt of Yahweh's robe was perhaps evoked by the incense flowing outward from the altar along the floor of the temple. The winged creatures called seraphim were perhaps the ornate figures adorning the temple lectern. The temple choir singing the Sanctus sounded to Isaiah like the company of heaven singing the praises of God ceaselessly to one another. And as the trumpets rang out during the great enthronement ceremony, it seemed to him as though the very foundations of the world were being shaken.

Isaiah, quite understandably, was afraid. It was as if he were no longer sitting in the congregation of the temple in eighth-century B.C. Jerusalem, but had been lifted to the very centre of heaven itself. As the size of this fact dawned upon him, his feelings of awe and wonderment began to give way to a sense of profound unease. What was the purpose of this meeting? Devout Jews since the time of Moses had believed that no one could come into the presence of God

and live. To be confronted directly by the immediate appearance of
Yahweh was in effect a sentence of death (see Exodus 19: 21). Now
face to face with his own judgement, Isaiah was overcome with the
fear of his own uncleanness, and his lack of readiness at this early
point in his life to meet death. Moreover, he knew that he shared in
the sinfulness of his society, and dreaded the words he was to hear:

> Woe is me! I am lost, for I am a man of unclean lips and I dwell
> among a people of unclean lips; yet with these eyes I have seen the
> King, the Lord of Hosts.

What happened next was totally unexpected. Instead of receiving
judgement he received forgiveness. The experience — perhaps the
moment of absolution in the liturgy — seared itself so deeply into
Isaiah's soul that he later described it as a touch on the mouth by a
burning coal. He was freed from his sins with such piercing strength
that the sense of release made him almost faint, and then filled him
with enormous joy:

> Then one of the seraphim flew to me carrying in his hand a glow-
> ing coal which he had taken from the altar with a pair of tongs. He
> touched my mouth with it and said: "See this has touched your
> lips; your iniquity is removed, and your sin is wiped away."

This was the moment of Isaiah's conversion, and with a sudden
infusion of grace he understood its meaning as a call to prophesy
before the people of Judah. His mouth had been seared and cleansed
in order to speak forth the words which the Lord God would give
him. In something akin to a religious trance, he heard God's voice
addressing him and found himself responding by offering his life.

> Then I heard the Lord saying, "Whom shall I send? Who will go for
> me?" And I answered, "Here am I, send me."

This vivid and wonderful account points us to the power of
liturgy. It points us to the fact that God comes to meet us in these ancient and powerful rituals without any human foreknowledge or
understanding. Isaiah's experience, for all its strangeness, is not
unique. Many believers since his day have turned to worship when

they have sought the Lord. In his book *The Shape of the Liturgy*, Anglican monk and liturgical scholar Gregory Dix has eloquently expressed the universal character of this repeated experience. Commenting on Jesus' command to "do this," he writes:

Was ever another command so obeyed? For century after century, spreading slowly to every continent and country and among every race on earth, this action has been done, in every conceivable human circumstance, for every conceivable human need from infancy and before it to extreme old age and after it, from the pinnacles of earthly greatness to the refuge of fugitives in the caves and dens of the earth. Men have found no better thing than this to do for kings at their crowning and for criminals going to the scaffold; for armies in triumph or for a bride and bridegroom in a little country church; for the proclamation of a dogma or for a good crop of wheat; for the wisdom of the Parliament of a mighty nation or for a sick old woman afraid to die; for a schoolboy sitting an examination or for Columbus setting out to discover America; for the famine of whole provinces or for the soul of a dead lover; while the lions roared in the nearby amphitheatre; on the beach at Dunkirk; while the hiss of scythes in the thick June grass came faintly through the windows of the church; tremulously, by an old monk on the fiftieth anniversary of his vows; furtively, by an exiled bishop who had hewn timber all day in a prison camp near Murmansk; gorgeously, for the canonization of Saint Joan of Arc — one could fill many pages with the reasons why men have done this, and not tell a hundreth part of them.

Here we catch a glimpse of the importance of liturgy. For millions of Christians through the centuries it has been the meeting ground with God, the holy ground on which the faithful have stood before the Lord of life. Every celebration of divine worship contains the possibility of a transforming encounter with the God of grace and glory. Every event in which the people of God gather in ceremonial praise, no matter how simple or how splendid, is an occasion for the discovery of that deep communion with Christ that leads us into a new and redeemed fellowship. Every act of corporate prayer is filled with the potentiality of the sudden revelation of God, and the breaking open of time and space that masks the presence of the Holy One.

No individual can participate in a celebration of the liturgy without the possibility that, on this particular day and in this particular rite, the day of salvation will arrive for him or her. The liturgy is a way God has arranged for the salvation moment to happen. It is a vehicle for the soul to be transported to the very centre of the divine life. For countless millions of individuals, the liturgy has, at some moment or another, become the Mount of their Transfiguration.

This is so whatever liturgical rite may be in use on a given day. Though liturgy is in the end a human work, its unique character consists in the fact that God meets us in and through the actions of the worship. It is God who makes possible the encounter. Because the impetus and direction of revelation is always from God to us, no particular style or form of words created by human ingenuity can manipulate or force God to disclose himself. All human endeavours to penetrate the mystery of the Creator, all earthly attempts to summon forth the divine presence, are of themselves ineffectual and powerless. The miracle of liturgy is that God chooses to be present to us and graciously permits the self-disclosure, and no barriers of words or understanding are too great for God to bridge.

It follows then that all liturgy, whether traditional or contemporary, can be a vehicle for divine grace and human transformation. Liturgical reformers have never claimed to be creating better avenues to God. The reasons for liturgical change are, as we shall see, much more modest. It is exasperating, therefore, to observe men and women who consider themselves to be devout believers staying away from the church's celebrations because of objections to the particular rite in use on a certain day. This is an example of the mistaken devotion which assails people on both sides of the liturgical fence from time to time. What is sad about such pseudo-martyrdom is that, when one cuts oneself off from celebration and worship, one also closes off an opportunity to meet with and be met by the Lord of life. This can hardly count as a demonstration of faith.

Two Models of the Church

There are, however, many devout Christians for whom liturgical change is nevertheless difficult. In the congregation I presently serve there is a surgeon whose family I visited shortly after I was appointed as rector of the parish. They were, I discovered, thoroughly committed to the church. We had a pleasant and interesting evening, and at the end of it the conversation turned to the new services. David was deeply attached to the Prayer Book. He had come into the Anglican church as a child, and had found more and more beauty in the traditional liturgies as he grew older. During our discussion he said: "Please understand that I'm not against change. In my profession I have to cope with rapid change every day. In fact, it's just because of this that I look for something else from my church. When I come on Sundays I like to see the candles in exactly the same place on the altar, and to sing the same hymns and say the same words that are familiar to me from my childhood."

In the same congregation, sitting not far away from David and his family on Sundays, is a woman of 83 years of age. She has been widowed for over 20 years, and I well remember my first visit to her. She has bright eyes, a clear mind, and exudes a transparent faith in Christ, to whom she prays daily. She told me about her past, her years of church attendance, first at Sunday school and then as a young married woman. She had been the local president of the A.C.W. at one time, and still did a lot of knitting and collecting of clothes for the northern clergy families. In all the years as a member of the church she had never been particularly excited by the services. Then when the contemporary rites were introduced, she gradually began to enjoy herself. She explained: "As I get closer to death, I find I'm getting passionately interested in life. There's a lot of life in the new services. Church today feels freer and more joyful than ever before, and it helps me cope with myself. I don't want to go backwards. I want to grow and to change. So long as I'm changing, I know I'm alive."

What separates these two points of view is obviously not age, nor something as simple as individual taste. Though neither of them would put it this way, the difference between them has to do with their understanding of the church. Theologians and scholars have long discussed questions of the nature and purpose of the church, and regularly trade papers on the subject, but in my experience as a pastor the large majority of ordinary Christians operate with only two models of the church, or two *ecclesiologies* to put it technically, and it is these which come into conflict around the issues of liturgical change.

The first might be called the island model. The argument for it goes something like this. The church is meant to be an island of stability and permanence in a troubled and changing world, a sanctuary of tranquility and spiritual peace, a haven from the tumult of worldly life. The church should be slow to change, or at the very least should examine change critically and not be blown about by every passing wind of newfangled doctrine. In a period of both religious and moral decline, moreover, it is all the more imperative that the Christian tradition be preserved and maintained, and that there be no capitulation to the fashions of secular society, such as the rush towards modernization and so-called relevance. A variation on this sentiment may be found in the circles of the educated and among some of the *literati*. The church, they say, must preserve the beauty of its ancient language and the dignity of its solemn liturgies. These too are part of our spiritual heritage, and must be handed on to the generations which follow us.

There is a long and established history behind this ecclesiology. It can be traced back into the Old Testament. At its root, the prophetic tradition was a conserving tradition which continually called the people and their leaders back to the terms of their covenant with God and to the ancient truths of their faith. The prophets fought long and often unsuccessfully against the tendency in Israel to adapt religion to the surrounding culture. Indeed, they saw the causes of the nation's frequent troubles as originating in the headlong rush to emulate the lifestyle, culture, and beliefs of the neighbouring peoples, and in the subsequent dilution of Israel's worship. They argued for a distinct and separate religious culture among the people of God.

One of the greatest reforms in the history of Israel took place during the time of Jeremiah, after the discovery of the Book of Deuteronomy which had lain hidden in the temple wall for many years. The book laid out strict principles for the ordering of religion and society according to the covenant made between God and the people at Mount Sinai. It was a conservative reform which attempted to restore true and uncorrupted worship to the nation. The preservation of this worship was associated with the preservation of Israel. Each was seen to be consequent upon the other. The drift towards the absorption of other cultural and religious influences into Jewish devotion would, it was thought, quickly lead to national destruction.

This prophetic tradition in the Old Testament, though radical in its pursuit of social transformation, was conservative in its insistence on the preservation of the traditional liturgical forms and the ancient ritual observances. Thus, despite its remoteness from the twentieth century, it expresses a theology which still resounds in the contemporary church. Anyone who is attempting to introduce liturgical change in parishes or dioceses must therefore deal sensitively and respectfully with this well-grounded theological position.

Many Christians, on the other hand, find themselves drawn towards a second model of the church. This is quite different from the first, and evokes quite separate liturgical needs. It might be called the pilgrim model. The argument for it goes like this. The church is called to be a pilgrim people moving through history, seeking God in new ways in changing times. Though steeped in the wisdom of tradition, it must remain open to new insights and developments both in the church and in the world itself. It should not become static, preserving archaic forms, but should strive to be faithful, willing to risk the unfamiliar in the belief that God is revealed in the new as well as the old. It should encourage fellowship, not just piety, and be engaged in building new relationships, particularly relationships of justice, between people.

This point of view, like the former, also has a firm basis in scripture and church history. Its roots could be uncovered in the "exodus" theme which runs throughout the Old and New Testaments. God's deliverance of the Hebrew slaves set them free to move into a new and creative era of their history. For many years they wandered as a nomadic people, seeking an understanding of God and their new destiny. They were propelled out of a lifeless and static situation into one where their dependence on God increased, their faith was deepened and made more dynamic. In the New Testament, the exodus theme continues. God acted at Easter and Pentecost to deliver and set free the people. The resurrection of our Lord and the sending of the Holy Spirit meant a new exodus for the church, a going out into the world with much uncertainty and risk to bring the good news of Jesus Christ to others. Obviously, the pilgrim model suggests that the time is ripe for a new exodus in the church today, a revitalized search for a dynamic relationship with both God and the world involving a renewal in worship, evangelism, and mission.

Now these two ecclesiologies are not the same. One is institutional, the other organic. One stresses the conserving role of the church, the other its transforming role. In one, truth and doctrine are fixed and clear, in the other they are in process of being revealed by God. One embraces traditional worship with its dignity and rich associations, the other finds contemporary worship more liberating and appropriate. To the adherents of the first view, the other kind of church seems unstable and insecure. To the second, the first view appears close-minded and hidebound. How can both views co-exist?

Continuity and Change

These two models contain important elements for our understanding of the nature and purpose of the church. Each expresses an aspect of what we are called to be. For the church to be faithful it will have to contain both positions in a conscious tension. Christians must live with the paradox of having to encompass both stasis and change, conserving what has been revealed to us as gospel and life, and at the same time allowing ourselves to be broken and renewed so that the world may be transformed. The complexity of preserving the substance of faith while risking new forms of faith's expression is no easy matter to grasp, and demands the best efforts of every Christian. We must avoid building the type of church which is so stable that the gospel is stultified. And we must avoid the uncritical modernism that is so innovative that the gospel is diluted. Both stability and change are vital to growth.

Liturgical change presents an opportunity for those who have only partially grasped the nature of the church to move out of a partial and one-sided entrenchment into a more imaginative and creative equilibrium. We therefore need to avoid being pressured by one side or the other to adopt a single-minded approach to worship. For the rest of this century at least, Anglicans will have to live with two liturgical styles in the church. No one should be forced to renounce traditional rites for contemporary ones or vice versa. Rather, we need to learn to live with each of them side by side, in a conscious and deliberate ambiguity. This means, for the time being at least, accepting both tradition and innovation in worship willingly and open-mindedly, seeking what is spiritually valuable in each.

Mutual acceptance of differences in liturgical styles is not a betrayal of either the Prayer Book or the alternative rites. It is an exercise in tolerance, perhaps the cardinal Anglican virtue. From the beginning, our church has had to blend together opposing theologies and ecclesiologies. The history of the first Prayer Books is a history of the struggle between Catholic and Protestant interpretations of the nature of the church. The genius of Anglicanism has always been its resistance to extremes and its ability to find a creative synthesis between opposing positions in a way that remains faithful to the great catholic tradition of Christianity. The compilers of Anglican liturgical rites have constantly sought to balance the demands of doctrinal purity against the requirements of ecclesial unity. Their success is what constitutes our contribution to the larger church.

Christianity is a living tradition. The worship of the church in all times and places reflects this. From the time of the great social and religious reform during the ministry of Jeremiah, to the Day of Pentecost, through the turmoil of the European Reformation up to the Liturgical Renewal Movement of the present century, the church has continually sought to present its faith in God in a fresh and vital way through its celebration and preaching. One of the costs of belonging to a living tradition is that we have to balance the demands of both continuity and change. The church at every moment in its life is in tension between the unchanging gospel and the changing world. In order to live creatively and faithfully in this ambiguity, we have to come to terms with the living nature of the tradition in which we stand. We have to grasp and accept the fact that change is part of being alive. It may help to realize that this is as true of the past as it is of the present.

The Changing Prayer Book

It was for the purpose of renewal and change that the Prayer Book was originally written. Never intended as an eternal and absolute book of rites, it was, in fact, amended many times. The early years of the Church of England were characterized by many upheavals in liturgy. It was a time of theological and political ferment. Brilliant efforts were made to modernize and revitalize the church's ritual life, but as monarchs changed so did the Prayer Book. During the course of Anglicanism's first century the rites of the church were revised drastically five times. The first editions were dated 1549, 1552, 1559, 1604, and 1662. More recently, an attempt was made to change the Prayer Book in England in 1927, but the effort suffered defeat in the British Parliament. Other provinces in the Anglican communion have also introduced revised editions of the Prayer Book, notably Scotland (1637, 1764, and 1927), the United States (1789, 1892, 1928, and 1977), Ireland (1877), South Africa (1929), India (1933), and Canada (1918 and 1959), In the present period of liturgical change, therefore, it is worth bearing in mind that the traditional rites are hardly fixed and firm.

The preface to each revision of the book explains why it was thought fit to permit alterations, variations, and amendments. The reasons were then as they are now. They were an effort to provide new rites and ceremonies for the church in its contemporary situation, to utilize the best and newest translations of the scriptures, to enable the people of God to worship in the common tongue, and to equip the faithful for ministry, mission, and evangelism. The preface to the 1622 edition, quoted at the beginning of this chapter, expresses confidence that any reasonable enquiry into the purpose of the new rites can be answered with satisfaction. The *Book of Alternative Services* can make this claim also, for it stands in the same living tradition as its predecessors.

To understand how the *Book of Alternative Services* is designed for the contemporary situation, with what elements of continuity and what amount of change, we must first examine the context of the church in the late twentieth century and see how different it is from the context assumed by the authors of the various Prayer Books of the past.

Questions for Discussion

1. Share your feelings about liturgical change. How do you feel about the prospect of having both traditional and contemporary styles of worship? (Note: let each person in the group speak briefly without challenge or debate.)
2. What particular liturgical celebrations have been significant for you? Describe (or write down privately) some moment when you experienced God personally in a service of worship.
3. What is your operative model of the church? Are you an islander or a pilgrim or do you have some other model?
4. What tensions exist in your parish around the subject of liturgy? How does your community try to deal creatively with them?

2. How the World Has Changed

The Church of the present day is continuous with the Church of the sixteenth century, but different, just as the Church of the sixteenth century was continuous with but different from its mediaeval roots. (from the introduction to *The Book of Alternative Services*)

Liturgy and History

Liturgy is always contextual. That is, it is an expression of the self-understanding of the church at any given point in history. This is no less true of the ancient rites of the church as it is for the contemporary ones. The worship of Christians in every age is a response to God's will and purpose for the church in the concrete circumstances of that particular time and place. Liturgy is not the same as scripture. There are good reasons why the church does not amend or add to the Bible, for we believe it contains all things necessary for human salvation without the need for alteration. But liturgy is not in this category. It is and must be a living expression of the encounter between the unchanging gospel and changing history.

There have been several watershed moments in history to which the church has had to adapt. In each of them, both theology and worship have evolved in new ways to reflect the faith and the needs of Christians in the new era. One of them was in the fourth century when, after the conversion of the Emperor Constantine, Christianity became the official religion of the Roman Empire. Prior to this, the liturgical character of the church had been essentially that of a house movement, but from the fourth century on liturgy grew from the style appropriate to small informal gatherings to that of grand public ceremonial in large and splendid buildings. Another was in the sixteenth century, when the church precipitated the great cultural upheaval of the Reformation and there emerged new structures and liturgies along denominational lines. A third is in the twentieth century, when the secularization of Western culture has pushed Christianity aside from the central position it has occupied in social and political affairs since Constantine, and has created a new situation of marginalism for the church.

It is with this third era, and its spiritual needs, that the *Book of Alternative Services* is concerned. It represents the liturgical response of our church to the changed cultural and political circumstances, as well as the new theological climate, of contemporary history. The watershed through which we are passing is the shift from Christendom to post-Christendom. The era that began with the conversion of Constantine, and which lasted from the fourth century to the nineteenth, spanning the great divide of the Reformation, has met its death in our lifetime. Religion and religious symbols no longer provide the basis of our culture. Science, economics, and technology have become the new social paradigms, the basic models by which people today think of themselves and their situation. Spiritual matters are now regarded generally as secondary to these more material issues, and the credibility of religion itself is under doubt in many secular quarters. The church no longer exists in the historic social, political, and intellectual climate which produced the Prayer Book. We are no longer at the centre of culture. Modern Christians, in fact, are post-Christendom Christians.

In order to appreciate this shift, and to understand the context of the *Book of Alternative Services*, let us first look at six important historical changes that have emerged in the last hundred years. Let us compare the situation of the post-Christendom church with that of its ancestor.

Christendom

1. *Church-State Relations.* Throughout most of the Christendom era the church enjoyed a comfortable interdependence with the state. In the early years, Christianity was an important element in the unification of a diverse and far-flung empire. Constantine and his successors required a uniform faith to integrate the scattered and often competing tribal components of their imperial domain. Theological and doctrinal differences — which had existed in the church from apostolic times, starting with the controversy over circumcision in the days of Saint Paul — were suppressed with the full force of civil law. Doctrinal shadings and contending schools of theological

belief, which today we would call denominations, were branded as heresies. An orthodoxy was sought by the great councils of the church which was then imposed upon all citizens with the sanction of the state.

By the time of the Reformation, when the Prayer Book was written, the political scene in Europe was much more complex. By the end of the Middle Ages the once unified empire was fragmented into separate, autonomous nation states, particularly in northern Europe. In fact, the Reformation was made possible in large part because of the desire in these states to assert their political autonomy. The break from Rome by both Protestant and Anglican reformers could not have been achieved without the support of secular authorities. Martin Luther's execution, for instance, was prevented only be the patronage of some of the German nobility.

In England we find the clearest example of state-supported church reform. The emergence of our tradition in Christendom is a result of the desire by both secular and ecclesiastical leaders in that country to be free from external domination. When Henry VIII declared himself the supreme head of the Church in England, it was from a complex variety of motives (not just his divorce) in which both church and state saw an advantage. For the king it was an opportunity to resolve the centuries-old struggle for control of church wealth and taxation, and for unimpeded authority to govern the country. For the church it was an opportunity to end some of the long-standing decay in its theological and liturgical life, and to respond to the exciting innovations of the continental reformers. The English Reformation happened precisely because of the close interdependence of church and state. It was a revolution undertaken with mutual profit. From that day to this, the monarch and Parliament in England have had a central role in governing the church, including the formulation of its liturgy.

2. *Political Centrality of the Church.* In exchange for protection by the state, the Christendom church was given a place of central involvement in national affairs. State religion developed in most European countries. Established churches enjoyed privileges and rights denied to excommunicate factions or dissenting religious minorities, and in return for this status, the dominant churches lent their moral and spiritual weight to the secular powers. After the demise of the

Roman Empire, the church was the only unifying political structure on the divided continent, and retained its acquired power in social and economic matters well into the late mediaeval period.

Ecclesiastical and political goals were intertwined during Christendom (those who are wont to complain today about the church's involvement in politics have little sense of history). The Crusades and the Inquisition are dramatic examples of the ability of the church to launch vast social movements with secular backing. Senior bishops in England were given special places in the upper chamber of Parliament, from where they could influence government policy. On a less grand scale, the political power of the church touched the lives of ordinary citizens on a daily basis. The levying of taxes, the large land holdings, the deference which had to be paid to the senior clergy, and, in some places, the exemption of clergy and religious from prosecution under the civil law for any crime, all reveal the privileged position the church was accorded in those years.

3. *Europeanization.* As the continent became Christian, so also there took place a process of reverse acculturation of the Christian faith. All the early creeds and doctrinal formulations, by which the great councils of the church defined the content of Christianity, were expressed in the framework of European thought. The terms in which Christians came to be taught the doctrines of the Trinity, the humanity and divinity of Christ, of salvation, of the authority of the church and so on, were all cast in a Greek philosophical mode of language and logic. Augustine provided the first great monument of Christian theology in terms of Neoplatonism. Later, Thomas Aquinas delivered a comprehensive and systematic statement of doctrine under the influence of Aristotle. Both endure still in Western seminaries, providing the rational foundation of all subsequent Christian thought.

The practical effect of this intellectual and theoretical acculturation of the faith became evident only during the later period of colonial and missionary expansion. In teaching the faith to new converts, little distinction was made between Christian belief and European cultural habits. Canadian Indians, for example, were prevented from speaking their own languages, and traditional native spirituality was suppressed. Evangelism of aboriginal peoples meant the dismantling of their cultural traditions and ancient patterns of thought, as well as of family life, and the substitution of white European values. In more resilient cultures, such as that of North Africa, for instance, the logic and customs of European society were able to gain only a fragile foothold, and were easily swept away by the tidal wave of Islam, which claimed a more Semitic identity. Hinduism in India successfully resisted effective penetration by missionary Christianity for the same reasons.

4. *Ptolemaic Cosmology.* During the era of Christendom, scientific thought was not immune from the considerations of church doctrine. The second-century Egyptian astronomer Ptolemy had suggested that the earth was the fixed point in the universe, around which revolved the stars and planets, including the sun and moon. This theory accorded well with the biblical understanding of mankind as the crown of creation, and became official church teaching. The sixteenth-century Polish astronomer Copernicus, however, received much different treatment. His studies showed that the true relation of the stars and planets indicated the sun to be the fixed point in the cosmos. Almost a century later, Galileo confirmed this. But his teaching was officially repudiated, his books suppressed, and Galileo himself was imprisoned. It was many years before the leadership of the church acknowledged its mistake and retired from making scientific pronouncements.

The widespread assumption that man and the earth were at the centre of things shaped many aspects of religious and secular life. It encouraged a feeling of superiority and pride. Men and women came to think of themselves as the highest work of God's creation, the sum and fulfilment of the purpose of the universe. It was an easy step for a church steeped in a Europeanized theology to make the further assumption that, as the planet was the centre of the cosmos, so the church was the pinnacle of human aspiration and achievement. Christian (and European) thought and practice were believed to be the necessary condition for the betterment of all peoples. Ptolemaic cosmology gradually induced a Ptolemaic theology.

5. *Rejection of World Religions.* During the pre-Christendom era, the church had frequently found itself the victim of religious intolerance. The Book of Acts tells how the apostolic community was subjected to harassment by the Jewish authorities and intellectual challenge by the Greek philosophers. With the acquisition of tem-

poral power after Constantine, however, the church sought to establish its claim to universality both by repressing the Jewish religion, and by developing the doctrine of salvation in an exclusive way. It was taught that there could be no salvation outside the church. The Christian religion was proclaimed the sole repository of revelation and truth, and other religious traditions were condemned as pagan and erroneous.

In a time when there was little communication between the great regions of the world, it is not surprising that Christian theology should develop a poor understanding of other religions. There is also an inherent necessity in all religious thought to express a universal world-view (one should never bother with a faith that offers a merely partial and relative view of reality). The scope of theology is broad and encompassing, and this is no less true of other major religious traditions than it is of ours. However, this Ptolemaic theology, like its earlier scientific counterpart, began to come under question towards the end of the era. The broad search for global community in modern times has opened new avenues of dialogue between the world's religions and a new sensitivity among Christians to people of other faiths. This is evidence of the end of a long and formative epoch, and the emergence of a new outlook in a new world. Such openness was intellectually difficult, not to mention legally dangerous, in the Christendom era.

6. *Denominationalism.* The early part of Christendom was characterized by the suppression of breakaway groups and the enforcement of orthodoxy. Theological thought was not suppressed, however, and the church then as now did not lack fruitful and inventive minds, each contributing to a rich matrix of intellectual challenge and debate. But once a doctrine was pronounced as official teaching, usually at one of the great councils, it could not be gainsaid without dire penalty. It was when the church lost the power to enforce uniform belief, after the rise of political nationalism at the end of the mediaeval period, that the emergence of separate and autonomous churches took place. When the Reformation got under way, the different denominations defined themselves by issuing doctrinal statements and by creating unique and particular liturgical rites.

The Prayer Book is one of these. It was produced in a time of religious upheaval and is an avowedly denominational document.

Its genius consists not so much in the beauty of its Elizabethan language, as in the way it succeeded in expressing the unique identity of Anglicanism as a *via media* between Catholicism and Protestantism. But for this reason it inescapably reflects the polemics of the Reformation disputes. When the authors of the Prayer Book wrote what they did, they were consciously trying to differentiate Anglican faith from all the alternatives. Other Christian churches were doing the same thing, of course, and consequently each developed a separate liturgical identity. Intense emotional loyalties have accompanied these denominational identities, and their liturgical expressions, throughout the period of Christendom. The modern mind has tended to become impatient with this rivalry and competition, and many new Christians are exasperated at the divisiveness this has introduced into the body of Christ.

This is a brief sketch of the Christendom era. Though conditions varied from place to place, and the pendulum of privilege and power tended to swing back and forth, nevertheless these general categories applied almost everywhere. The church enjoyed a unique relationship with other institutions such as government, the universities, and the arts, which has been profoundly formative of our thinking and outlook in the twentieth century, and which has irrevocably influenced the development of Western culture. Much that is good and worthwhile in our present time results from the creativity of this era. Christianity has inspired some of our greatest art, music, and literature. The emergence of democratic rights and freedoms, and many aspects of social ethics, have their roots in Christian moral theology. Hospitals, schools, and many of the caring organizations we now take for granted in our modern social infrastructure have all evolved into state-supported institutions after starting out as religious ones.

The Prayer Book reflects this era both implicitly and explicitly. It assumes the outlook and priorities of a state-supported church. It calls upon its members to maintain their civic duties and responsibilities, to observe peacefulness and tranquility for the glory of both God and the sovereign, and warns heretics and evil-doers of the perils of the state sword. Prayers abound for the king or the queen's majesty as much as for the majesty of God, and the advancement of the overseas colonies and dominions is inseparably associated with the advancement of the kingdom of God. Other religious traditions, particularly the Jewish, are regarded as mired in darkness and error, and the salvation of the world is imagined in terms of the worldwide dominion of the church. All cultures and civilizations other than that of Europe are assumed to be inferior, and the central place of mankind in the grand design of creation is untarnished by any scientific doubt.

The Prayer Book has survived in the church and nurtured its generations only so long as the world from which it came has survived. As that age passes away, so also passes away that understanding of the church's life and mission. There has arisen in this century a need for new theological perspectives and new liturgical resources which will express the situation of Christians in a way that fits their new and different context. But this is no easy task. For many of us it is difficult to accept that the end of Christendom has indeed come. So much of what it achieved is part of what we now are. Many of our religious attitudes and structures, and much of our worship, still show its influence and do not yet reflect the age into which we are moving. But what age is that? Let us take a look at six contrasting characteristics of the contemporary world.

Post-Christendom

1. *Church-State Separation*. Though there are still established churches around the world, the relationship between church and state in our time is not what it was during Christendom. The United States has enshrined the principle of the separation between church and state in its constitution, and Canada has followed the practice by convention. Even in Europe, the establishment status of many churches is strained and showing signs of terminal illness (witness, for example, the anger of Mrs. Thatcher at the refusal of the archbishop of Canterbury to conduct a victory service after the Falklands War). Christians, particularly clergy, may no longer claim special privileges or protections from secular authorities or the civil law. Indeed, the perception dominates many political corridors that the church is to be treated as simply one special interest group among others. In practice, this frequently means we are not to be taken too seriously.

The 1985 ruling by the Supreme Court of Canada striking down the Lord's Day Act is an instance of the shift in both the religious make-up of this country and the demise of Christian privilege. Our new constitution guarantees freedom of religion to men and women of all faiths. In an increasingly multicultural and multifaith society, the ceremonies and festivals of one particular religious group (even ours) cannot any longer be used as a basis to regulate the activity of the general population. The judgement caused little scandal among Christians. There is already a new perception of the social role of the church among many of its members. Liberated from the entrapments and dangerous compromises of power, the church has an opportunity to recover its apostolic mission. Part of that mission involves a new theology of church-state relations, as well as the recovery of a prophetic ministry. The *Book of Alternative Services* offers a clear and positive approach to this (see below).

2. *Political Marginalism.* Almost the only exemption from civil requirements now left to religious organizations is the tax-free status of buildings. Clergy are still excluded from jury duty in most courts, but may witness passport applications, and in general enjoy more exclusions from civic responsibility than access to its advantages. This is not a lament but an observation. The decline of Christendom has meant a new political role for the church and its leaders, one which is similar to the pre-Constantinian situation of the early Christians. They, like we, had to approach the centres of power from the outside, armed only with the weapons of moral persuasion plus whatever constituency support that could be mustered.

The freedom this creates for the church is already apparent. It affords us the opportunity to be among the marginalized and the outcast. It opens up the possibility of entering into the situation of Jesus, who demonstrated a particular compassion for the poor and victimized. Stripped of power, Christians are discovering for themselves the experience of the powerless, the majority of the world's population for whom the gospel is intended. With this discovery there is dawning a new understanding of the gospel message, a new theology of hope, and a broader vision of the kingdom of God. These are major elements in the *Book of Alternative Services*, as we shall see.

3. *Indigenization.* When the Christian gospel was taken out of continental Europe, where it had matured and developed, its cultural accretions became evident: choirboys with ruff collars, imported pipe

organs, a ponderous Anglican chant based upon some ancient recording from King's College, Cambridge — in, say, a Caribbean island context, where all the natural rhythm and colour of the local people was excluded. This is increasingly no longer the case. Post-colonial churches throughout the world are beginning to sift through the imported cultural elements of Europe which are not dimensions of the gospel, and to replace them with local cultural elements. Many provinces of the Anglican communion are developing structures of church life and forms of worship more appropriate to their own un-English circumstances. This process, known as indigenization, involves relating the ministry and mission of the church to the local context. Liturgically, for example, it means using locally familiar forms of language, music, and movement to enhance the people's worship. It assumes that religion is always involved in culture and that each can enrich the other.

Indigenization, however, means more than borrowing elements from the local culture to enhance the liturgy. It means entering deeply into the questions and issues of that particular society and allowing these to illuminate, and be illuminated by, the gospel of Jesus. This requires a new approach to theology and the church's classical statements on doctrine and faith. Samuel Amirtham of the church of South India writes:

> In India, for example, we have theological colleges which spend most of their time answering questions which European theologians have raised. Even where there are people struggling for their lives some schools go on with their teaching as if these struggles didn't matter. There are schools in Africa which act as if racism had nothing to do with theology, schools in Asia which seem to believe that poverty is not a concern for them. (Quoted in *One World* March 1985)

The process of indigenization is drawing attention to the urgency of an appropriate form of mission. As the churches become aware of their context, as well as of the universality of the gospel, they are being drawn into greater engagement with local issues such as poverty and injustice, which is the context in which millions of Christians live. The publication of the *Book of Alternative Services* in Canada is a dimension of this. It is an expression of the Canadian church's understanding of its mission. It attempts to articulate how the worldwide mission of the church finds expression in our particular situation. The book is designed to provide a continuous link with the liturgical traditions of the past while situating our worship in the unique geographical and cultural context of Canada today. To that extent, it is an indigenous collection of rites, although as we shall see, it also reflects the growing consensus of the Ecumenical Movement, and challenges the Canadian church to see its place within the wider context of the church throughout the world.

4. *Relativity and the Expanding Universe.* As Ptolemy gave way to Copernicus, and he to Galileo, and he to Newton, so our modern understanding of the universe is dominated by Einstein and the quantum theorists. No doubt these too will pass away, but whatever direction science now takes we are no longer able to imagine ourselves at the centre of the cosmos. Without possessing any detailed knowledge of these theories, contemporary men and women have come to an awareness of the vast complexity of creation and our limited place within it. For those without religious faith this has precipitated a sense of cosmic insecurity, perhaps best expressed in Nietzsche's vision of the death of God and the world unchained (chillingly described in his *Joyful Wisdom*). But even for those who continue to place their confidence in the Lord, the prospect of the extinction of life on the planet, now a technological possibility, has generated a new attitude of humility, and also a new reverence for creation.

Science itself, like the church, has lost some of its earlier triumphancy. The influence of positivism, so long the dominant philosophy in post-Enlightenment scientific method, has waned markedly as scientists become more aware of the mystery and inexplicability of life, and of the unavoidably hypothetical nature of much scientific theory. There is a growing openness in science to the integrity of religion, and by the same token a growing willingness among Christian scholars to learn from the expanding field of scientific knowledge. Scientists are less confident in making statements about the meaning of the universe, and theologians about its physical origins. Where religion and science conflict, it is usually bad religion and bad science.

The *Book of Alternative Services* avoids the old scientific-religious disputes by affirming the traditional biblical faith in God the Creator without taking any position on the method of creation or on the sequence and timing of the unfolding of the atoms. One of its significant contributions to the liturgy of the church in a scientific and technological age is the restoration of an attitude of wonder and thanksgiving for the beauty of the natural order and reverence for the things of the earth. (See the section on this below.)

5. *Inter-Faith Dialogue.* The World Council of Churches, significantly, does not use the term "non-Christian religions." Rather, it speaks of the "world's religions" or "other living faiths." The change in terminology is important, for it reveals a new attitude of respect for the spiritual dignity of other members of the world community. This is necessary as the church strives to play a constructive role in the building up of trust and mutual responsibility amidst the present climate of international hostility and suspicion. Religious divisions have been among the most tragic and bitter in human history, and there is a growing awareness among Christians that, if we are to be faithful to the God who calls us to the work of reconciliation and peacemaking, then dialogue has to replace condemnation as the basis of Christian approaches to other faiths.

Where dialogue is genuine, and not merely a deceit to proselytize, it is involving Christians in an examination of old doctrines of salvation and of the place of the church in the total mystery of God's redemption of the world. There is emerging in theology a new appreciation of the distinction between the church and the kingdom of God. The latter is a broader reality than the former, and raises the question of whether the fullness of God's revelation to the church in the person of Jesus Christ is necessarily diminished by the possibility of salvation beyond the church. It raises questions about the possibility of the bringing in of the kingdom through other traditions. These questions are in the process of being asked, and are hardly yet capable of being answered. For this reason, the *Book of Alternative Services* takes no radical position on the doctrine of salvation, but does avoid the imperialism of Christendom attitudes to other world religions. The position of the new rites on this question is explored in chapter seven.

6. *Ecumenism.* The post-Christendom era has been characterized by a new search for unity among various Christian churches. There are several reasons for this. The grounds on which the churches

separated in the sixteenth century have increasingly receded into history. None of the main protagonists of the Reformation exists today exactly as it did then, and some of the old barriers have disappeared with the attrition of time. Also, the colonial period brought missionary denominations into direct conflict with each other in ways that were often confusing and unhelpful, both to the task of evangelism and to the recipients of these distant and foreign theological distinctions. After the nineteenth century, as the churches realized this, they sought to minimize their conflicts for the sake of the gospel. In today's educated climate, theological jostling among separated Christian bodies seems increasingly wrong and out of place.

Today Christians in all branches of the church are becoming more conscious of what we hold in common as members of the body of Christ. The Faith and Order Movement of the early part of the twentieth century, which was a foundational element in the creation of the World Council of Churches, began the task of healing the wounds left by the Reformation disputes and the centuries of religious wars that followed. As time has gone by, the intellectual framework itself within which the old arguments were fought has slipped away. Biblical scholarship and the development of new kinds of systematic theology have created new problems and new areas of debate, which tend not to follow the old denominational lines.

Canada is uniquely situated to play an important role in the ecumenical age. Our history has not been dominated by religious wars to the same extent as Europe, and the size and geography of our nation has tended to produce a co-operative rather than competitive spirit among Christians. Inter-church coalitions are an important and unique feature of Canadian religious life. Today, the major churches in Canada work together on many issues: world development education, support of aboriginal land claims, human rights, pollution, monitoring overseas investments by Canadian corporations, as well as acting jointly wherever possible in making presentations to various levels of government. These actions represent a display of unity among the politically marginalized which holds much promise for Christian unity in other parts of the world.

This is a brief sketch of post-Christendom. It may perhaps now be seen how different is the situation of the modern church from its Constantinian and Reformation ancestors. Though there are points of connection with Christendom, there are many points at which the new context more closely resembles the situation of the pre-Christendom church. We are once again facing an indifferent and sometimes hostile world. We are once again at the edges of power, discovering a new mission among the powerless. There is no reason now for triumphancy other than the fact that we are still a vessel of the gospel message. But that is what energized the apostolic church. The need of the post-Christendom church is to recover the enthusiasm and energy of that era. We require a faith which empowers us to live creatively and faithfully in a minority situation, in a diverse and pluralistic society. It would be too much to expect new liturgies to do this. But without new liturgies it will be more difficult.

Let us now begin to see how the *Book of Alternative Services* responds to the needs of the post-Christendom church, and how it attempts to shape us for new life and witness in both continuity with and distinction from the Prayer Book.

Church and State in the *Book of Alternative Services*

The new rites continue the Prayer Book practice of offering prayers and intercessions for those in secular authority, but there is a difference today. Instead of an emphasis on the civic duty of the people to obey the monarch, we find the focus on strengthening and guiding political leaders to serve the people. Thus litany 5 reads:

> Let us pray for this country, and especially for Queen Elizabeth, the Governor General, the Prime Minister, and all in authority: the Lord help them serve this people according to his holy will.
>
> Lord, hear our prayer.
> (*BAS* p. 114)

Obviously, this slight but significant shift in emphasis reflects the changed nature of the political stucture in the contemporary world. We live in a democracy in which the role of the monarch is quite different from the days of the Reformation, more directed toward the constitutional oversight of governments and the symbolizing of national unity. We elect our political leaders and expect them to serve the interests of the people. We have had enough experience of corruption and misdirection in high office to know that wisdom and benevolence are not automatic virtues in those seeking elected positions in government, and although the Prayer Book authors knew this as well, they were not so foolish as to admit the thought into public worship. Today it is more possible to pray for wisdom and a spirit of service among those in authority over us, and indeed it seems appropriate to do so.

It is also apparent that political leaders have international as well as national responsibilities in a complex and interdependent world. We expect our leaders to play a constructive part in seeking the peace and well-being of the whole human community. Where the Prayer Book prayed only for the welfare and advancement of the sovereign's overseas dominions and urged the proper oversight of those working in the plantations, the *Book of Alternative Services* prays for all international leaders and for justice and peace among all peoples:

> For Elizabeth our Queen, for the Prime Minister of this country, and for all who govern the nations, that they may strive for justice and peace, let us ask the strength of God.

> Lord, hear and have mercy.
> (*BAS* p. 116)

The importance of seeking justice and peace rather than the selfish aggrandizement of empire in the dangerous climate of the nuclear age is expressed repeatedly in the new prayers and intercessions:

> Almighty God,
> kindle, we pray, in every heart the true love of peace,
> and guide with your wisdom
> those who take counsel for the nations of the earth,
> that justice and peace may increase,
> until the earth is filled with the knowledge of your love.
> (*BAS* p. 124)

We shall come back to the theme of peace and justice in chapter seven. Meanwhile there are some very "Prayer Book" prayers for the state in the new rites. We have not abandoned the long-standing Anglican tradition of taking pride in our form of government and in the quality of leaders with which God has frequently endowed us. This intercession is borrowed almost verbatim from the 1662 version:

> Strengthen your servant Elizabeth our Queen in true worship and holiness of life, be her defender and keeper, that she may always seek your honour and glory, and endue the leaders of this nation with wisdom and understanding.
>
> Hear us, good Lord.
>
> Bless and defend all who strive for our safety and protection, and shield them in all dangers and adversities.
>
> Hear us, good Lord.
>
> Grant wisdom and insight to those who govern us, and to judges and magistrates the grace to execute justice with mercy.
>
> Hear us, good Lord.
> (*BAS* p. 139 – 140)

The last bidding about mercy is an addition to the old prayer. There was a marked stress on justice in the old rites, but it was conceived largely in terms of meting out punishment to evil-doers. The new rites soften the severity of those words and add the balancing virtue of compassion, encouraging the judicious treatment of offenders in a spirit of fairness and mercy.

There is also a softening of the strong nationalistic tone of the Prayer Book. Where it would praise the virtues of English culture and civilization in implicit assumption of its global superiority, the *Book of Alternative Services* takes a more cautious approach to national identity (very Canadian). The prayer for responsible citizenship in the Occassional Prayers reveals a pride in our nation and people, but lacks megalomania:

> Lord, keep this nation under your care. Bless the leaders of our land, that we may be a people at peace among ourselves and a blessing to other nations of the earth. Help us to elect trustworthy leaders, contribute to wise decisions for the general welfare, and thus serve you faithfully in our generation.
> (*BAS* p. 678)

The attitude toward the state in the *Book of Alternative Services* thus reflects an aspiration for responsible participation of all the people in its affairs and decisions, and does not limit the role of leaders to the enforcement of order and the pursuit of national interests alone. It stresses the mutual accountability of leaders to people and vice versa, and of all the nation to God. It urges a servant role upon those in power, and points all people in high office and low to their membership in the community of nations and to the importance of actively pursuing international stability.

Christian Unity

Unity among Christians is an important feature of the *Book of Alternative Services* in both obvious and not so obvious ways. Its not so obvious ecumenism has to do with content and shape. First, the new rites are built around the framework of the ecumenical lectionary (pages 262 – 431). This lectionary, initially the work of Roman Catholic scholars, is spread over a three-year period. In other words, it starts to repeat itself every third year instead of every single year as did the Prayer Book. This means that a far greater portion of scripture is covered in the new rites than was formerly the case in Sunday worship. Also, where the Prayer Book allowed only two readings on Sundays, using mostly the New Testament and calling only sparsely upon the Old Testament during the year, the new lectionary includes three readings, one of which is almost always from the Old Testament or Apocrypha. The three lessons usually contain a particular theme which suggests a focus for the liturgy of that day. The intention of these amendments is twofold. On the one hand, it is hoped to generate greater familiarity among Anglicans with the Bible as a whole, instead of with selected passages. And on the other, it is hoped that Christians of all denominations will eventually move to these common readings so that there is a measure of unity among our separate liturgical identities, and a common focus each Sunday in each liturgical community.

Secondly, the new rite for the eucharist reflects growing international agreement on the shape of the liturgy. Ecumenical scholarship has uncovered much more detail about the worship of the early church than was known to the authors of the Prayer Book, which was based upon the more diverse and elaborate liturgies of the late Middle Ages. These early rites show a general uniformity of shape, and it is this which the *Book of Alternative Services* restores. For those congregations which still prefer the language of the Prayer Book, there is a form of the old rite starting on page 230 which is re-arranged according to the more ancient order. A comparison of the shape of the old Prayer Book rite with the one in the *Book of Alternative Services* will reveal the difference. It is important to remember that the *Book of Alternative Services* uses the early rites of the church as its basis (see the detailed explanation on pages 179 – 180). Many Anglicans imagine that the services in it are new, and indeed many of them are, but the shape and much of the content of them is ancient, more so than the Prayer Book itself. By making this change, our church is bringing its liturgy closer to the practice of the wider church, and thus moving us away from some of the partisan polemics implicit in the Reformation rites.

The obvious ecumenism in the book is evident in many of the prayers and collects. Perhaps the clearest example of the new mood for unity in the church is expressed in the propers for the Conversion of Saint Paul (January 25). The prayer after communion reads:

> Gracious God,
> you filled your apostle Paul
> with love for all the churches.
> May the sacrament we have received
> foster love and unity among your people.
> (*BAS* p. 401)

That's explicit enough. The collect for the Sunday between October 2 and 8 (proper 27) expresses the same hope:

> Almighty God,
> you have built your Church
> on the foundation of the apostles and prophets,
> Jesus Christ himself being the chief cornerstone.
> Join us together in unity of spirit by their teaching,
> that we may become a holy temple, acceptable to you.
> (*BAS* p. 384)

The careful wording of this prayer merits attention. It asks God to join us together in unity of spirit and through apostolic teaching.

This is quite different from praying for some sort of structrual or institutional union among all the churches. While that may be a distant goal for the future, it is so distant that it is absent from the *Book of Alternative Services*. In the present climate of interchurch co-operation, it is enough to pray for growth and development in the things which unite us, such as our common witness and continuing dialogue. This in itself is a sign of movement, and little would be served by asking for more than is achievable at this stage in the ecumenical debate.

The prayer after communion on the Sunday prior to this also expresses a careful hope. It asks God to draw Christians together into a sacramental fellowship. As we leave the altar to go out into the world, the prayer reminds us of the goal of eucharistic unity among all Christians. It looks for the day when we may all share in a common witness as the fruit of the mystery of bread and wine:

Father in heaven,
strengthen the unity of your Church,
so that we who have been fed with holy things
may fulfil your will in the world.
(*BAS* p. 383)

The sharpest and most strident reminder of the sinfulness of continued division within the body of Christ, however, comes in the meditation provided for Good Friday. Where the equivalent liturgy in the English Missal makes no mention of the scandal of disunity, the Good Friday anthem in the *Book of Alternative Services* minces no words:

I sent the Spirit of truth to guide you,
and you close your hearts to the Counsellor.
I pray that all may be as one in the Father and me,
but you continue to quarrel and divide,
I call to you to go and bring forth fruit,
but you cast lots for my clothing.

Holy God, holy and mighty,
holy and immortal one, have mercy upon us.
(*BAS* p. 315)

In these visible and invisible ways, the *Book of Alternative Services* offers us a vision of a unified body of Christ, joined together in sacramental fellowship and acting in common witness. It moves us beyond the denominationalism of the older rites towards the hoped-for future reconciliation between our divided and too frequently competing separate traditions. It points the church towards the time when it may be possible to celebrate the fulfilment of our Lord's prayer for his disciples, that we might all be one (John 17: 21).

Reverence for Creation

While the Prayer Book certainly contains moments of praise and adoration for the beauty of the earth, particularly in the Harvest Thanksgiving festival, it is hardly a consistent theme throughout the book. People of the sixteenth century had a greater sense of the rhythms and seasons of nature, being a predominantly agricultural people, than do the urbanized Christians of the modern era, and perhaps for this very reason saw less need to express their awe and wonder at nature in their liturgies. Apart from the very long and very lovely canticle *Benedicite, Omnia Opera* (*BCP* p. 26), offered as an optional addition at Morning Prayer, there are sparse opportunities for thanksgiving for the earth's beauty in the old rites other than at harvest time and at the Rogation festival before Ascension Day (*BCP* p. 199).

Perhaps because the fragility of life on the planet has become an issue in the twentieth century, and perhaps also because the urbanization of the church in many parts of Canada has removed us from direct contact with the land and its seasons, the *Book of Alternative Services* contains a major emphasis on creation and on the responsibility of mankind to be its stewards. The old Benedicite does appear, but it is called *A Song of Creation* to make its purpose clearer, and it is split into three parts, to be used separately on different occasions (*BAS* p. 82 – 84). Harvest Thanksgiving also appears, as do the prayers for Rogation, but here the emphasis is much more sharply focused on our responsibility for the preservation of the earth's bounty:

Creator of the fruitful earth,
you made us stewards of all things.
Give us grateful hearts for all your goodness,

and steadfast wills to use your bounty well,
that the whole human family,
today and in generations to come,
may with us give thanks for the riches of your creation.
(*BAS* p. 396)

Reverence for the creation is closely connected with reverence for
life, and the *Book of Alternative Services* makes a good effort to
affirm the dignity and value of all created life. In a wonderful new
addition, it provides the following responsory to be said or sung
after one of the lessons at Morning or Evening Prayer:

You send forth your spirit, O Lord;
you renew the face of the earth.

   You send forth your spirit, O Lord;
   you renew the face of the earth.

O Lord, how manifold are your works!
in wisdom you have made them all;
the earth is full of your creatures.
   You renew the face of the earth.

All of them look to you
to give them their food in due season.
   You renew the face of the earth.

You give it to them; they gather it;
you open your hand, and they are filled with good things.
   You renew the face of the earth.

May the glory of the Lord endure for ever;
may the Lord rejoice in all his works.
   You renew the face of the earth.
(*BAS* p. 108)

Responsories are poetic arrangements of biblical material, in this
case from Psalm 104, meant to be recited antiphonally by a cantor
and the people. This one praises the life-giving nature of the Spirit. It
is appropriate for the Pentecost season or for any festival where the
theme is life, beauty, fruitfulness, bounty, and so on. It is one instance among many of the focus in the *Book of Alternative Services*

on the importance and value of created life, and on the Source of life who comes to meet us in worship. So central is this theme that it has been incorporated into two of the six eucharistic prayers. In prayer 5, for example, which is intended for use at special family or children's services, we read:

> We give you thanks and praise, almighty God,
> for the gift of a world full of wonder,
> and for our life which comes from you.
> By your power you sustain the universe.
> (*BAS* p. 204)

The words are simple, appropriate for a liturgy celebrated in the presence of small children, but the image is profound. It is expanded in prayer 4:

> At your command all things came to be:
> the vast expanse of interstellar space,
> galaxies, suns, the planets in their courses,
> and this fragile earth, our island home;
> by your will they were created and have their being.
>
> Glory to you for ever and ever.
>
> From the primal elements
> you brought forth the human race,
> and blessed us with memory, reason, and skill;
> you made us the stewards of creation.
> (*BAS* p. 201)

This prayer lifts our minds to contemplate the wonder of the expanding universe. It reaches into the area of scientific cosmology. It is the most startlingly modern of all the amendments to the eucharist, but it expresses in a carefully crafted way both the biblical affirmation of God the Creator, and the scientific affirmation of the evolving nature of life. It places God at the centre of existence, not mankind, and reminds us of our place as stewards of the gifts of the earth and of the skills and talents we possess that are capable of affecting the continuation of life, skills that we are called to use responsibly. The imagery of the prayer locates the human race within creation as another aspect of its glory, rather than as the reason for its existence, but thereby manages cleverly to evoke both cosmic realism and at the same time spiritual optimism. It is a prayer that could not have been prayed by any generation previous to ours.

God's judgement on the sinful use of the earth's resources is also an aspect of the new liturgies. The spectre of ecological collapse, the misuse of renewable resources, waste and pollution by industries and consumers, all are included in various penitential litanies and acts of confession. The great litany of penitence on Ash Wednesday, for example, asks:

> For our waste and pollution of your creation, and our lack of concern for those who come after us,
>> Accept our repentance, Lord.
> (*BAS* p. 285)

This also could not have been confessed by any generation before ours. The rites recognize both the goodness of God and the destructive capacity of mankind, and attempt to combine both a joyful attitude to the beauty of life with a respectful sense of its fragility and vulnerability to human greed and blindness. The creation theme will be an important element in the worship of the post-Christendom church, and is an aspect of the new spirituality of the *Book of Alternative Services*, which will be explored later.

Canadian Content

Although the *Book of Alternative Services* has been produced in partnership with other churches involved in liturgical renewal, it is nevertheless an Anglican document and a Canadian one. While the Prayer Book was distinctly English in origin, with few revisions being made in the 1959/62 edition to bring home the rites other than to include the Governor General and the provinces in the state prayers, the new rites reflect the process of indigenization in this country. Again, there are some visible and not so visible ways in which this is done.

First, the book recognizes that in a nation so regionally diverse and geographically vast there is unlikely to be one uniform order of worship that will satisfy every part of the church. One of the reasons why the 1980 General Synod instructed the Doctrine and Worship Committee to prepare a set of alternative rites was that the rigidity and uniformity of the Prayer Book, with its limited options and repetitiousness, was no longer by itself able to accommodate the plurality of liturgical needs within Canada. Thus, the new rites include a much-expanded range of alternative prayers, canticles, litanies, responsories, lections, and calendar observances in order to provide for the wide variety of practice and devotion within the Canadian church. The customs and traditions of individual congregations differ from place to place, as do the demands of particular pastoral situations. Accordingly, there are in some cases whole alternatives provided to specific liturgical rites, such as the funeral service which occurs in three forms (see p. 565 – 598), as well as within the rites themselves. This flexibility, which is confusing at first but becomes familiar with usage, is intended to respect the diversity of our church while at the same time providing a common order and unity.

Secondly, provision has been made wherever possible for the rites to be conducted by lay persons, if necessary. Many parts of Canada are not served by ordained clergy, and the principal ministry in these places is performed by lay readers or others authorized by the bishop. A glance at the rubrics (the stage directions in red print) will indicate where a service may be conducted by a lay member of the church, and where a bishop or priest must officiate. The pastoral offices in particular are services which may appropriately be conducted by a non-ordained person, for instance, the Ministry to the Sick or the Ministry at the Time of Death. Unless an ordained person is specified, the term *celebrant* in the *Book of Alternative Services* includes authorized laity as well.

Thirdly, the calendar provides for the commemoration of persons who have particular significance in Canadian life, or in the history of a local area or region. As well as including the usual list of saints and worthies, it honours those whose witness of faith has enriched our national Christian heritage. The list is not vast, but it is interesting:

January 12	Marguerite Bourgeoys	Educator in New France, 1700
	John Horden	Bishop of Moosonee, 1893
March 10	Robert Machray	First Primate of Canada, 1904
April 2	Henry Budd	First Canadian native priest, 1850
August 30	Robert McDonald	Priest in the western Arctic 1913

September 4	First Anglican Eucharist	celebrated in Canada, 1578
September 10	Edmund James Peck	Missionary to the Inuit, 1924
October 19	Jean de Brébeuf and companions, 1642-49	
December 31	John West	Missionary, the Red River, 1845

The Calendar (see pages 15 – 33) is not strikingly obvious to the general membership of the church, and is not observed closely in many parishes other than for the principal seasons and festivals, but it is an instance of the indigenization of worship and mission, and the attempt of the Canadian church to claim and celebrate its own national identity separate from that of the Church of England. For that reason alone it represents a significant advance over the Prayer Book.

More visibly and obviously, the new rites include prayers and intercessions specifically for the nation, its industries, and people. Not surprisingly in a resource-rich land, the principal industries for which prayers are offered are fisheries and agriculture (future editions should perhaps include mining). Some examples of these national prayers appear above, but the best example is the prayer for Canada in the Occasional Prayers:

Almighty God, you have given us this good land as our heritage. May we prove ourselves a people mindful of your generosity and glad to do your will. Bless our land with honest industry, truthful education, and an honourable way of life. Save us from violence, discord, and confusion; from pride and arrogance; and from every evil course of action. Make us who came from many nations with many different languages a united people. Defend our liberties and give those whom we have entrusted with the authority of government the spirit of wisdom, that there may be justice and peace in our land. When times are prosperous, let our hearts be thankful; and, in troubled times, do not let our trust in you fail. (*BAS* p. 678)

This prayer acknowledges the multicultural reality of Canadian society, and manages carefully to honour the varying backgrounds of its people, including both native and immigrant Canadians. It recognizes the regional and linguistic tensions within the country, and attempts to rise above them by calling us to unity in the midst of our plurality. It gives thanks for the extraordinary wealth of natural and human resources which enrich our lives, but points us away from arrogance and pride at our fortune toward the proper use of these gifts for good. It is a lovely prayer which succeeds in bringing together many of the elements we have been considering: unity, justice, reverence, service, and responsibility, and it expresses the Canadian context in the multicultural uniqueness of our people.

No doubt the book will take on more of the characteristics of an indigenous church when it is translated into French and into the principal native languages. That will take many years. In the meantime, however, it is a beginning. The Canadian Anglican church now has a set of rites produced largely on domestic soil.

To conclude, in Tennyson's phrase, "the old order changeth, yielding place to new, and God fulfils himself in many ways." We no longer live in the age of Constantine or the Crusades, nor indeed of Henry, Elizabeth, or Cranmer. The era which saw the golden age of European Christianity and produced the *Book of Common Prayer* is gone, and though some would still prefer to bask in its afterglow, the task of the church today is to be faithful to God and to make known the love of Christ in the contemporary generation. To do this it needs to think new thoughts and to re-order its life.

The Prayer Book was a product of its time, just as the new rites are a product of ours. It assumes and reflects a Christendom perspective within its pages just as the *Book of Alternative Services* points us to a new post-Christendom world. This new age, similar in many ways to the context of the early church, requires Christians to live with a vigorous and renewed missionary spirit, with a stronger concept of belonging to an historic religious community, and with a joyful and sustaining spirituality. Nostalgia for the past is understandable but inappropriate. When nostalgia becomes schizophrenia — entrenched commitment to living in the twentieth century as sixteenth-century people — then it is positively destructive. Our living tradition needs to remain alive.

Questions for Discussion

1. Do you agree that we have entered post-Christendom? What do you find positive about this? What do you find negative?
2. In many parts of the world the church retains great political power. Is this an advantage or a disadvantage in proclaiming the gospel?
3. How do you feel about the movement towards Christian unity? Should this affect the way Anglicans worship?
4. Do you think "a collection of indigenous rites produced largely on Canadian soil" will make any difference to Canadian Anglicans?

3. Community

Baptism is the sign of new life in Christ. Baptism unites Christ with his people. That union is both individual and corporate. Christians are, it is true, baptized one by one, but to be a Christian is to be part of a new creation which rises from the dark waters of Christ's death into the dawn of his risen life. Christians are not just baptized individuals; they are a new humanity. (from the preface to Holy Baptism: *The Book of Alternative Services*)

Community and Society

One of the most important social developments of the last 100 years has been the shift from the village to the city. Most of us today live in or around the great urban centres of Canada. Those of us who do not have, nevertheless, come to rely increasingly on the supply of goods and services from the distant cities which make rural or northern life more comfortable.

This shift from village to city has brought significant changes to our modern way of life. German sociologist Ferdinand Toennies describes this as the movement from community to society. In a study called *Gemeinschaft und Gesellschaft* published in 1885, he pointed out that the large majority of contemporary men and women are now growing up in the context of society (*gesellschaft)*, whereas our forebears had grown up in the context of community (*gemeinschaft*). The distinction is worth exploring.

Communities are small. They are made up of people who are bound together by a common ancestry or a common history. They tend to be close-knit, and often difficult to join if one is an outsider. They have a pride in their own distinctiveness. People who live in communities feel a strong sense of belonging. They are united with one another through a complex web of shared traditions and common values. Members of a community are frequently marked by a strong communal identity, that is to say, they experience themselves primarily as parts of a whole rather than as isolated individuals. Thus the experience of leaving a community can often lead to personal crisis and loss of self-identity, if one has no other community to move to. We may say, therefore, that communities tend to conserve relationships and to generate in their members a mentality of inter-connectedness. For this reason, they are often slow to change and can be constrictive of individual freedom. Few communities tolerate individual deviation from the established norms.

Most communities have a centre. Sometimes it is a crossroads of some sort. In close proximity to one another, there are usually shops and homes, centres of commerce, and people's places of work. In many rural communities, the church has a central location in the community and plays a prominent role in the life of its members. In some parts of Canada one frequently finds a graveyard in the grounds of the church — reminding the living of the abiding presence of their ancestors, and providing a symbolic memorial to community tradition.

Societies, on the other hand, are large and spread out. They are made up of people who have no common ancestry but rather a pattern of diverse and separate histories originating in many different places. They tend to be pluralistic and scattered, presenting no barriers to movement or integration, and welcoming people from many backgrounds. People who live in societies often find themselves searching for smaller units or communities to join, for the larger group is too vast to provide a clear sense of identity or belonging. These people have few shared traditions or common values. Instead, their common bonds tend to be economic. Society is a complex web of interrelated interests, rather than beliefs, and so the unifying focus is provided by a common concern for material well-being, political differences emerging only around different means to the goal rather than around the goal itself. People tend to think of themselves as isolated units, separate components of an amorphous and indistinct whole.

Thus societies tend to promote a mentality of individualism. Members define themselves by what they possess rather than where they belong. The quest for personal happiness and success dominates the social agenda. The world is perceived as a place to be exploited, as a field of opportunity for personal advancement. But the paradoxical outcome of this is that society weakens identity.

People shaped by this environment can often experience life in disconnected ways. Many of them have lost touch with their personal and communal roots. Whole industries of counsellors and psychologists have arisen to help people find themselves again in the impersonal urbanized context of modern society.

Society has no centre. It is perhaps symbolized by the modern freeway with its off- and on-ramps, slicing through the city and dividing it into compartments and zones of separate activity. In one zone is a housing suburb, in another an industrial park. Somewhere away from the residential areas are the commercial shopping zones with their vast parking lots, and farther still is the downtown core where most people go to work. Churches cling to the suburbs, with a few downtown congregations often struggling to draw people in, and the cemeteries are out of sight, erasing the communal memory. The life of the society dweller is compartmentalized. S/he lives in one part of the city, works in another, shops in another, and is separated from other members of the family by perhaps many hours of driving. Modern man and woman belongs nowhere. Little wonder, therefore, that we are experiencing in the post-Christendom age a new search for community.

Liturgy and Community

The Prayer Book assumes an age of community. It does this so naturally and unconsciously that one can fail to notice how the assumption permeates its pages. The tradition of the calling of banns of marriage, for instance, arises from a time when all records of births, deaths, and marriages were kept by the church. When John Smith from village A desired to marry Mary Brown from village B, the clergy in both villages were required to announce the fact on three successive Sundays at the main service of worship. Naturally, most members of the respective villages would be present. If there were any legal impediment to the marriage (if, for instance, John Smith already had a wife in village C) someone would almost certainly know. Communities have no secrets. In this way, the sanctity of marriage was upheld, and the moral standards of the people maintained.

Revisions to the 1959 Prayer Book of Canada, as well as the rites in the *Book of Alternative Services*, reflect the different circumstances of society. Although banns may still be called as a courtesy, most clergy today are unable to ensure that couples coming to the church to be married are free of legal impediments, and therefore require them to obtain a marriage license.

Where the Prayer Book assumes an age of community, however, the *Book of Alternative Services* does not. The new rites have been deliberately created for the more fragmented and less homogeneous society, for a time in which Christians are in a minority, and where it cannot be taken for granted that all persons living within parish boundaries will seek the rites of the church at major transition points in their lives. The contemporary liturgies are designed to equip the post-Christendom church to strengthen its own sense of being a community, and to help us bring new members into the church in ways that help them experience a new identity in Christ. They are an attempt to respond to the obvious need among many alienated people to find secure, caring relationships that will provide the stability and support necessary for purposeful living.

The *Book of Alternative Services* engages the modern church in the intentional building up of its sense of identity and community life. Let's take a look at some of the ways it does this.

People of God

First, the new rites feature significantly the theme of the people of God. We are encouraged to think of ourselves not only as individuals but as a people, not only as isolated souls striving for healing and salvation, but as members of a community which God has chosen and called together for the healing and salvation of the world.

The concept of the people of God is a biblical one, originating with the call of Israel to become a chosen nation in covenant relationship with God, and continuing with the call of the disciples to form a faithful community in the company of Jesus, and with the strong sense of mutual service and fellowship which bound the apostolic church together after Pentecost. Both the Old and New Testaments make clear that God's way with men and women is to call them out of isolation and separation into new partnerships, so that they may be sent out together in loving service and ministry to the scattered and the lost. Furthermore, the scriptures indicate that salvation is

God's promise to persons-in-community rather than individuals-in-isolation. Whenever the gift of redemption is announced, it is to the people of God as a whole. In fact, there is little biblical support for those modern armchair Christians who pursue a purely individualistic piety in complete separation from the Christian community.

The tendency to claim loyalty to the Christian faith while remaining apart from the church is a relatively new heresy, one with which most of us are familiar today. It is a result of two things. On the one hand, it is an attitude encouraged by the individualism of modern culture, which applauds the pursuit of personal goals and pleasures, often without any accountability to the community. On the other, it is the result of the lingering influence of Christendom in the very different circumstances of post-Christendom. The church has clung to the belief that to be a member of society is to be in some sense Christian, and has therefore encouraged the casual use of its sacraments (such as baptism and marriage) without proper instruction as to their meaning and the commitment to the Christian community which they entail. The *Book of Alternative Services* discourages this sacramental laxity, and instead urges us to see our identity as primarily that of belonging to God's people.

Consider, for example, the invitation to communion in the eucharist:

The gifts of God for the People of God.
(*BAS* p. 213)

Here is a small but significant addition to the Prayer Book, which addresses its invitation to the congregation primarily in an individual way. In fact, it is in this new rite that we see the clearest examples of the New Testament emphasis on the eucharist as the constitutive celebration of the church. Just as the community celebrates eucharist, so the eucharist creates and sustains the community. In the *Book of Alternative Services* the eucharist is presented as the assembly of those united with Christ (the first words on p. 185 are "The Gathering of the Community") to be strengthened by the mysteries of his sacramental presence for corporate mission and witness. The point is stressed in no less than four of the six alternative eucharistic prayers:

Send your Holy Spirit upon us
and upon these gifts,
that all who eat and drink at this table
may be one body and one holy people,
a living sacrifice in Jesus Christ our Lord.
(*BAS* p. 195)

This prayer points us to the unity we share in Christ despite all the distinctions of race, class, income, and ability that separate us from each other in the world. At the communion table these differences are transcended and we become one people again through the power of the Spirit. Again, in eucharistic prayer 2 we read:

In fulfilment of your will
he stretched out his hands in suffering
to bring release to those who place their hope in you,
and so he won for you a holy people.
(*BAS* p. 196)

Here we see how the *Book of Alternative Services* relates the coming into being of the church with the atoning death of Christ. His death has given birth to our life, and has released us from the grip of despair, alienation, and separation to win for us a life of hopefulness, holiness, and freedom in the context of the religious community. The thought is continued later in the same prayer:

Gather into one
all who share in these sacred mysteries,
filling them with the Holy Spirit
and confirming their faith in the truth,
that together we may praise you
and give you glory.
(*BAS* p. 197)

This prayer expresses the idea of unity in terms of eucharistic fellowship. It points not only to the goal of unity between the churches, but also to the goal of unity within the congregation in each eucharistic community. We who eat and drink holy things are called out of our self-centred concerns and needs and pointed outwards to the needs of others in the wider church with whom we share the common cup. This sense of belonging to one another in the body of Christ, and of taking on mutual responsibility for those who share our faith and hope, is captured in eucharistic prayer 4 where our common baptism is made the focus of the renewal of the Christian community:

> We who have been redeemed by him,
> and made a new people by water and the Spirit,
> now bring you these gifts.
> (BAS p. 203)

Notice the prayer does not say that we have been made new individuals through baptism. It says we are made a new people. This is not intended to submerge individual and personal life in the body of Christ, as some totalitarian states endeavour to suppress individuality in favour of mass culture. Rather, it is intended to suggest that personal life includes the social, and is not achievable in isolation. Fully personal life is life in community, where our individual uniqueness is affirmed and accepted, and at the same time rendered responsible and accountable. We cannot be fully human by ourselves, and we cannot be fully members of the body of Christ in separation from the people he calls into being. The sentence spoken by the celebrant at the breaking of the bread sums this up in a simple phrase:

> Celebrant We break this bread to share in the body of Christ.
> People We, being many, are one body,
> for we all share in the one bread.
> (BAS p. 212)

People-making

As well as the obvious ways in which the new rites attempt to strengthen our sense of community by this emphasis on the people of God, there are some less obvious but no less significant ways in which they encourage this to happen. They have less to do with the words of the rites than with actions and symbols.

The first is the exchange of the peace. Most newcomers notice this addition to the eucharistic liturgy more than all the others, sometimes with some discomfort. This is understandable, for the older rites focused exclusively on the vertical relationship between the worshipper and God. We are not accustomed to the new emphasis on the horizontal relationship with our fellow worshippers, and some Anglicans are clearly unable to accept this as a valid and formative function of liturgy. To a great extent the reasons for this are cultural rather than theological. Ours is not a touching culture. We are taught not to make physical contact with other people, especially strangers, except in highly formalized and strictly governed ways — such as the compulsory handshake upon being introduced, or within the rules of contact sports. Touching is considered an intimate act in our part of the world, and its introduction into the liturgy has left many Anglicans scandalized.

Yet our Lord frequently used touch in the course of his ministry. Most of the healing miracles involved the laying on of hands. In fact, Jesus did the unthinkable in the cleansing of lepers — he placed his hands upon them. Lepers were considered repellant and untouchable in first-century Palestine, and Jesus' act of making physical contact was intended to bridge the human separation and alienation which they had experienced as much as to rid them of their disease. Further, there is some indication in the gospels that his relationship with the disciples involved the act of holding or physical greeting. When the risen Christ appeared to Mary in the garden on Easter Day, his first words to her were, "Do not touch me" — presumably because she was just about to. Also, in the later appearance to the eleven, he invited Thomas to place his hands into the wounds on his body to verify that he was not a phantasm or hallucination, but the same Jesus whom Thomas had touched before.

The exchange of the peace requires us to touch one another, and is a sign of the intimacy that ought to characterize the Christian community. Obviously, it needs to be done with sensitivity and mutual respect — no sudden grabbing or kissing or hauling people into the air. With complete strangers a handshake is all that is necessary, with friends an embrace, and with spouses and family members a kiss after the eastern manner, a touching of lips to both cheeks.

The kiss or exchange of peace is not meant to have romantic overtones (nor is it meant, in the deliciously understated words of the rationale in the Third Canadian Eucharist "to be a foretaste of the coffee hour"), but is intended to be an act of reconciliation and peace-making between members of the community. It arises from Jesus' statement in the Sermon on the Mount: "If you are offering your gift at the altar and there remember that your brother has something against you, leave your gift there before the altar and go; first be reconciled to your brother, and then come and offer your gift" (Matthew 5: 23 – 24). Since the eucharist is the memorial of our reconciliation with God through Christ, it is fitting that there be a moment in it when we can seek and offer forgiveness from and to one another. The ups and downs of life mean that most families need such occasions of reconciliation between members, and the liturgy provides this opportunity in a simple way.

The peace should properly come before the offertory, as the biblical verse suggests, and it does so in the contemporary rite — an example of the way in which the *Book of Alternative Services* restores the earlier shape of the liturgy, as mentioned in the last chapter. In the Prayer Book eucharist it comes at a bad moment for movement and greeting, occurring just before the communion, and therefore has tended to lose its original meaning. The peace is an act of people-making. Its purpose is to make reconciliation and forgiveness a concrete reality within the community of faith. To this end it calls us out of our personal isolation and encourages us to be members one of another and to risk discovering the healing power of touch.

Children and Liturgy

A second example of community-building in liturgy is the incorporation of children into worship. This has come about in large part through the recovery of the essential meaning of baptism through the work of the Liturgical Movement. Baptism, as the earliest practice of the church attests, is the full incorporation of individuals into Christ and into the Christian fellowship. In the sacrament of baptism we are buried with Christ in his death, and raised with him in his resurrection. Through it we are reborn by the Holy Spirit, and by it we are invited to participate in the feast which is a foretaste of the heavenly banquet. The eucharist is the privilege of the baptized.

This is so whatever the age of the baptized person. Infant baptism does not change the essential character of initiation into the Christian community. This, of course, has not always been so. At some indeterminate point in the Constantinian era, baptism was divided into two separate rites to be administered at different moments in the candidate's life: the water bath, administered shortly after birth, which cleansed and purified the candidate from inherited original sin; and the laying on of hands, administered at the age of "reason," which signified the anointing of the candidate and conferred the full rights and responsibilities of membership in the church. The latter act came to be called confirmation. It was a sacrament reserved exclusively to the bishops in the Western church (though not in the Orthodox churches, where it is widely performed by priests), and was withheld from infants until they could undertake a personal declaration of faith, confirming by themselves the vows that had been made on their behalf at the time of the water rite.

Most Anglicans were raised with this theology of initiation, for it is this practice which appears in the Prayer Book. The consensus among modern scholars, however — expressed, for example, in the *Baptism, Eucharist and Ministry* document of the Faith and Order Commission of the World Council of Churches (1982) — is that this tradition undermines the unity of the baptismal act by splitting it into two. The water bath and the laying on of hands are part of one and the same rite, and are not divided in scripture nor in the practice of the apostolic church. The original initiation sequence by which new Christians were led into the church was (a) baptism, (b) anointing, and (c) admission to the eucharist, all of which occurred together. If Christians are to move forward together in the "post" society, and if we are to achieve some uniformity in the matter of these sacraments — which have divided the church since the Reformation — then some common ground must be found on which to unify our diverse practices. The best basis for doing this appears to be the tradition of the (undivided) pre-Constantinian church. This, at least, is the conclusion of the *BEM* document. On theological grounds, therefore, there are strong reasons for admitting baptized children to the communion.

There are also other reasons. We have learned from the social sciences that young people learn best by experiencing rather than by merely observing. Education has undergone profound scrutiny in this century, and it is apparent from the researches of developmental psychology that the old passive-receptive methods of teaching are inadequate by themselves. Learning requires participation. The mere possession of facts does not of itself lead to understanding. This is as true of spiritual realities as it is of material ones. One of the important functions of liturgy is to form and to educate, so that members of the religious community may grow in the knowledge and love of God. This may be more realizable if members are encouraged to exercise their baptismal privileges as soon as possible.

From the educational point of view, the old approach to the admission of children to communion placed undue emphasis on reason and on the cognitive aspects of faith. These are important, to be sure, but they are not the whole of Christian faith. Our love for God, and God's love for us, are not strictly rational things, and are felt and experienced sooner than they are comprehended. Indeed, the latter cannot occur without the former. The experience of being included in the corporate fellowship, and of participating in its sacraments from a young age, will hopefully lead to an earlier appreciation of the inclusive and universal nature of God's love, and thus to a stronger Christian community. Besides, children already understand God in ways often lost or unlearned by adults. It was, perhaps, for this reason that Jesus welcomed children into his arms, and warned the adults, "I tell you this: unless you turn round and become like children, you will never enter the Kingdom of Heaven" (Matthew 18: 3). The adult community needs the children's gifts of innocence and faith, as much as the children need the adult's maturity and wisdom.

Thus, the *Book of Alternative Services* treats baptized children as members of today's church, not merely of tomorrow's. It does this principally through its assumption that children are part of every celebration of the church and are not excluded from participation by imprisonment in the crypt, and through its inclusion of a specially written eucharistic prayer designed for use at children's or family eucharists. In the Third Canadian "blue booklets" this appeared as eucharistic prayer 4. With the addition of an extra optional eucharistic prayer in the *Book of Alternative Services*, this has now become eucharistic prayer 5. It reads in part:

> We give you thanks and praise, almighty God, for the gift of a world full of wonder, and for our life which comes from you. By your power you sustain the universe. . . . You created us to love you with all our heart, and to love each other as ourselves, but we rebel against you by the evil that we do. In Jesus, your Son, you bring healing to our world and gather us into one great family. . .

in sending Jesus, your Son, to us you showed us how much you
love us. He cares for the poor and the hungry. He suffers with the
sick and the rejected. Betrayed and foresaken, he did not strike
back but overcame hatred with love.
(*BAS* p. 204 – 205)

The prayer carefully addresses some of the insecurities and
vulnerabilities of childhood (and adulthood!), and reassures the
hearers that they are enfolded in the loving care of Jesus by their inclusion in the great Christian family. It holds up the fascination of
young people for the new world as an occasion of praise and
thanksgiving, but confronts honestly the evil and darkness which
many experience and into which Jesus enters still. The simplicity of
the language is a deliberate attempt to reach those who cannot yet
appreciate the sonorous beauty of Elizabethan English.

In addition to this important recognition of children in the
eucharist, other prayers and intercessions are included specifically to
uphold the place of young people in the life of the church and in the
world. Thus, for example, litany 5 contains the bidding:

Let us pray for children and young people: the Lord guide their
growth, and development.
Lord, hear our prayer.
(*BAS* p. 115)

Also, as in the 1959 Canadian edition of the Prayer Book, the
Book of Alternative Services contains prayers for families to be used
at home, in a form allowing children as well as adults to exercise
leadership. Family prayers are an important aspect of a Christian
home, and daily or regular weekly prayer is helpful in the nurturing
of Christian attitudes and values among children (and among
adults), as well as being a fulfilment of our baptismal commitment to
"continue in the apostles' teaching and fellowship, in the breaking of
bread, and in the prayers." Further, the service of Thanksgiving for
the Gift of a Child expresses prayers of joy and gratitude that attend
the miracle of new life, and contains a significant new addition,
which will be of benefit to many Christian parents, in the inclusion
of a prayer for use at the birth of a handicapped child (see p. 613).

Participation

Newcomers to the Anglican church often remark how different the church is from what they expected. They frequently point to the level of participation in the new services, to the atmosphere of involvement they encounter on Sunday mornings. The church has a new feel to it. Sometimes, of course, this is a reason not to come back, but for the most part it adds a quality of interest and warmth to the liturgy which prompts further curiosity about the parish community itself. This curiosity, if it is received gladly by the congregation, can lead to a new relationship with Christ. Experienced love can bear fruit in an eventual profession of faith and renewal of life. The caring community, first experienced in the liturgy, can be an instrument of evangelism for those who do not yet know their need of God.

The different feel of the contemporary rites is not accidental, but arises from the deliberate attempt to involve participants in the celebration of the liturgy to a much greater degree. The reason for this is stated succinctly in the *Book of Alternative Services*, in the rubrics prefacing the Holy Eucharist:

> The celebration of the eucharist is the work of the whole People of God.
> (*BAS* p. 183)

The word *liturgy* actually means 'work,' in the same sense as *opus* which appears on music manuscripts or as a title adorning special artistic creations. Worship is an opus offered to God, a work of the human community, an expression of the community's faith and life. Sometimes, praise God, it is a masterpiece of beauty and human creativity, incorporating the highest achievements of art and music. Most often, it is a humble work, an offering of ordinary people in the context of their daily life and struggling faith. Liturgy is not the work of the clergy alone, and is not the exclusive preserve of the ordained, but rather it is the work of the clergy and people together.

The theological basis for this fact lies in the biblical idea of *laos* — the whole people of God. In the New Testament the word signifies all baptized Christians, all whom God has called into the church and to whom salvation is promised in Jesus Christ. *Laos* is not to be mixed up with the laity; rather, it encompasses both ordained and non-ordained Christians. Post-Christendom theology has recovered the notion of *laos* and with it a more apostolic understanding of ministry, particularly the authentic ministry of the non-ordained. More will be said of this later (see chapter six), but a consequence of its restoration in the church is the recognition of the distinctive roles of laity and clergy in worship.

Liturgy is the work of the *laos* over which the bishop or priest is called to preside. The new rites emphasize that the role of the celebrant is to be the "president of the assembly," the one who unifies and articulates the offering. The phrase implies that the liturgy itself is not his or her doing, but an opus which s/he is called to direct and orchestrate. It is the privilege of the bishop or priest to offer this work to God, but the work is done by the people. This has several implications.

Practically, it means that liturgy ought to be planned and prepared by a team of both ordained and lay members of the community. Worship committees are useful in this regard. If it is truly to reflect the people's offering, worship should come from a prayerful reflection upon the theme of the liturgical season by the people in the context in which it is to be celebrated. A worship committee, or liturgy group, enables the community as a whole to feel that they participate in liturgical planning. Also it provides a useful vehicle for clergy to feel the pulse of the community, and to plan worship that will be rich and joyful. The provision of many options and variations in the *Book of Alternative Services* really necessitates the discipline of planning, and provides the opportunity for discussion and the sharing of ideas by both clergy and people together.

There is another value in these bodies which may appeal to reluctant clergy. The introduction of new rites into a parish or religious community is an undertaking fraught with potential hazards. Clergy sometimes find themselves the object of resentment and anger, and conflicts often surface which can place the priest in a no-win situation. The starting of a worship group is a way to call people together for liturgical education, and offers a forum — outside public worship — for questions to be asked and answered. When a significant number of people have had an opportunity to raise their concerns and discover the rationale for change, they are then a powerful source of assistance to the priest in the introduction of new rites into the liturgical life of the whole church. Convinced laity are more persuasive in these matters than convinced clergy.

Besides the planning of worship, lay people are called to play a greater role in the liturgical action. Every community has a surprising pool of gifts and talents among its membership. Some are given the gift of music, some of reading, some of pastoral care, some of evangelism, some of teaching, some of organization and administration. The presider is exercising his or her gifts in the best manner when the talents in the community are utilized in appropriate ways in the liturgy, so that the worship is enriched and God is glorified. The skilfull presider is akin to a symphony conductor, carefully blending the assorted available spiritual gifts into the best harmony that particular group of people can produce. Musicians and liturgical artists should be consulted (not just told to do such-and-such), readers trained and selected, communion administrators appointed and prepared, and greeters and ushers organized. All this is encouraged by the new rites, which contain so many alternatives, options, and choices that only an unwise celebrant would attempt to plan worship alone.

Some have been given the ability to put the deepest feelings into words, and the astute presider will train them to offer intercessions on behalf of the community. The Holy Eucharist, in both the (contemporary and traditional) forms in which it appears in the *Book of Alternative Services*, provides for a lay person or deacon to lead the prayers of the people, and this is an effective moment to invite the participation of the people in the liturgy, for as the phrase suggests, more is intended here than the prayers of the clergy.

In addition to reclaiming the priest's role as presider at the assembly, the *Book of Alternative Services* provides for the traditional exercise of the deacon's role in the liturgy. The ministry of the deacon, as expressed in the Book of Acts, is to serve the pastoral needs of the community, to visit the sick, and to bring to the attention of the church the needs of the poor and downcast. This servant or diaconal ministry has been historically expressed in worship by the reserving of certain functions to the deacons, such as reading the gospel, preparing the altar for communion, receiving the gifts of the people, administering a chalice, and dismissing the faithful at the close of the service. The role of deacons in the church has been submerged by the ministry of priests in the last few centuries, and this is obvious in the Prayer Book, which largely overlooks this ancient order in its liturgical directions. The revival of the diaconate in the church, especially in areas of Canada where priests are in short supply, has led to a clarification of the distinct functions of priest, deacon, and laity in the liturgy, and this is reflected in the much more explicit directions given to each of them in the *Book of Alternative Services*. A glance at the rubrics in any of the rites will indicate this important development.

Preparation

Post-Christendom Christians are formed not born. Where once it was not uncommon for whole nations and tribes to be received into the church at a single occasion, and the central place of the church in the state guaranteed that most citizens would be baptized, this is no longer so. We live in a period of enormous religious ignorance and biblical illiteracy. Universities across the country are starting to offer introductory courses in the Bible so that literature students can understand the scriptural references and allusions permeating English classics (though not, alas, for any understanding of their spiritual content). Children in the public schools with no connection to the church often have little grasp of the original meanings of Christmas and Easter. Post-Christendom is characterized by religious reductionism, a watering down of the gospel message. (I recently came across a children's book written by Margaret Laurence in which the Nativity story is reduced to a tale about an interesting birth with some shepherds and animals standing around. The religious dimension of Christmas is totally removed, along with the name of Jesus.)

The privilege and responsibility of proclaiming the gospel in society, therefore, is now firmly ours. The good news of Jesus cannot be expected to filter through to everybody by some mystical osmosis. With historic tardiness, Anglicans and other Christians are slowly learning to recover the task of evangelism. As this happens, and as the Spirit leads people to approach the Christian community in search of new life, so we need to instruct these inquirers in the faith and life of the church, and to receive them into membership with adequate preparation in heart and mind.

Sacramental preparation, therefore, is one of the important emphases in the *Book of Alternative Services*. This is particularly so in the case of baptism, confirmation, and marriage. Before being admitted to these sacraments, candidates are to be instructed in their meaning and nature. There is nothing new about this, of course. The Prayer Book did not neglect the importance of teaching, by word and example, the faith of the church to newcomers. The Catechism is precisely such an instrument — albeit one based on a now discarded pedagogical method of rote memorization. What is new in the *Book of Alternative Services* is the suggestion that this be undertaken by the community as a whole and not simply by the clergy. Thus, for instance:

> The celebration of this rite of Holy Baptism requires careful preparation by both the community and the candidates. The service should take place when a congregation gathers for the principal Sunday eucharist.
> (*BAS* p. 146)

Since baptism is the supreme moment of personal entry into relationship with Christ, it is appropriately celebrated in the midst of the gathered community and in the context of the Sunday eucharist. Private baptisms held in the seclusion of an empty church on Sunday afternoons are an impoverished expression of this great sacrament of belonging. The practice was already proscribed by the revision to the 1962 Prayer Book in Canada:

> It is fitting that Baptism should be administered upon Sundays and other Holy–days at a public Service, so that the Congregation may witness the receiving of the newly baptized into the number of Christ's Church, and also may be reminded of the benefits which they themselves received and the profession which they made in holy Baptism.
> (*BCP* p. 522)

Whether of children or of adults, the preparation and baptism of new Christians presents a joyful opportunity for the renewal of congregational life.

Baptismal preparation can be done very effectively by a team of lay and ordained people working together with those who seek the sacrament. Theological instruction by the priest can happily be supplemented by the supportive nurture of other members of the community. The outcome of this is to build the new members into the body of the church from the very beginning, rather than simply developing their relationship with the clergy. In the case of infant baptism, a team of young parents gathered from the congregation is most constructive, for they can share their own experiences of the baptism of children with newcomers, and also act as models and examples of Christian parenting. In the case of adult baptism, an increasing trend in post-Christendom society, the congregation as a whole can be involved. Let me say more about this.

The practice of the early church was to receive adult inquirers into a special lay order called the *catechumenate*. The title means "those under instruction." For a lengthy period — sometimes lasting up to three years — the catechumens were introduced to the scriptures through study, they were taught how to pray, they were required to undertake works of charity in the world, and they were encouraged to experience the worshipping life of the community so they might be shaped into responsible witnesses to Christ. At each stage in the progress of the catechumens, starting with their first profession as "novices," they were brought before the whole body of baptized members and welcomed liturgically, prayed for, anointed, and assured of the community's commitment to their spiritual growth and well-being. Experienced elders from the church were appointed to assist the clergy in the training and instruction of the inquirers. These were called sponsors, the origin of godparents, and they were the ones who eventually presented the candidates at their baptism and vouched for their readiness and godly life.

This pre-Constantinian model of reception of new members has much to teach our post-Constantinian church. The length of a catechumenate need not be three years, of course. We must make realistic adjustments for modern society. However, many baptismal inquirers are unaware of the significance of what they seek. In my own congregation, members who participate in the baptismal preparation program are occasionally asked by newcomers to act as their sponsors — since many of them do not have any active or practising Christians among their circle of friends or in their family — and this has built some strong bonds of mutual support between experienced members and new Christians which is helpful to both of them. The revival of the adult catechumenate — with progressive rites of incorporation of the individual into the Christian community, culminating in baptism — is a development which will strengthen the unity and fellowship of the church, and help separate individuals to form a unified people.

Unfortunately, these rites are not yet included in the *Book of Alternative Services.* They are available only in the *Book of Occasional Services* of the Episcopal church (U.S.A.). The compilers of our new liturgies have included only the initiatory rites of baptism and confirmation in the green book, and intend to publish these occasional rites separately. This is an unfortunate omission, since the opportunities for community-building in the adult catechumenate are great, and will become increasingly necessary as post-Christendom wears on.

Incorporation

However, the rites of baptism and confirmation in the *Book of Alternative Services* do make exquisitely clear the nature of initiation as incorporation, that is, as entry into the body of the believing community. By these sacraments the individual is symbolically lifted out of his or her former life of alienation from God and isolation from the community of the Spirit, and brought into a new relationship with them. In place of a merely individual and separate identity the initiate becomes a participant in the historic identity of the people of God, whose roots and traditions go back to the very beginning of time and have evolved through the rich and elaborate rituals and ceremonies of the church to create a matrix of meaning for the person who seeks a religious purpose in life.

Where the Prayer Book simply and naturally assumed that people seeking baptism would enter the Christian community, the *Book of Alternative Services* makes this much more explicit, and moves the rite beyond the level of a social rite of passage, a merely cultural convention without any religious consequences, to the level of a visible commitment to Christ expressed, among other things, through participation in liturgy and prayer. Thus, for example, not only is baptism to be celebrated on Sunday morning (or at other principal occasions when the whole people of God are gathered for worship), but also during the course of the service the people are asked:

Celebrant Will you who witness these vows do all in your power
to support these persons in their life in Christ?
People We will.
(*BAS* p. 155)

This vow, which is new to the *Book of Alternative Services* (the
Prayer Book allowed no public participation other than that of the
parents and godparents), achieves two things. First, it reminds the
already baptized that receiving a new member involves their continuing support and affirmation of that person, so that he or she may
grow in the knowledge and love of the Lord. Secondly, it reminds the
newly baptized person (and their parents and sponsors) that the new
life in Christ involves participation in the liturgical life of the Christian community. The point is made even more explicit in the promises and commitments which follow:

Celebrant Will you continue in the apostles' teaching and fellow-
ship, in the breaking of bread, and in the prayers?
People I will, with God's help.
(*BAS* p. 159)

In other words, will you continue to live in the company of other
baptized Christians, to celebrate the eucharist with them, and to
develop in yourselves those spiritual disciplines which sustain Christians in their faith? Where the Prayer Book expressed baptism
primarily in terms of the salvation of the individual, the *Book of
Alternative Services* expresses it in terms of incorporation into the
community of the Holy Spirit, to whom God's salvation is promised.
The difference is significant, and it is intended to be a formative influence on the church in an age of religious decline and fragmenta-
tion.

The point is made again in the prayer of thanksgiving over water:

Now sanctify this water, that your servants who are washed in it
may be made one with Christ in his death and resurrection, to be
cleansed and delivered from all sin. Anoint them with your Holy
Spirit and bring them to new birth in the family of your Church,
that they may become inheritors of your glorious kingdom.
(*BAS* p. 157)

The prayer is carefully worded, expressing a theology of the church as an inheritor of the kingdom of God without restricting the kingdom of God to the exclusive inheritance of the church. As has already been mentioned, the *Book of Alternative Services* avoids a narrowly dogmatic position on salvation, and leaves to God the question of who is and who is not to be saved. The new liturgy does not make baptism a guarantee of salvation, nor does it restrict salvation to the baptized alone. It does, however, assert that through incorporation into Christ the baptized are invited to the heavenly feast at the end of time.

Again, the wording is careful. Baptism in the new rites is presented as an act of incorporation rather than of salvation. The latter is a gift of God, not of the church. The practical effect of this is to discourage the superstitious practice of bringing persons to baptism in search of "after-life insurance." Having people "done" for this reason is not the full meaning of baptism.

Confession and Reconciliation

The sacrament of penance is one many Anglicans associate with Roman Catholicism. But it has been one of the sacraments available in our tradition for centuries. The private confession of sin and the receiving of absolution is an act of restoration and renewal offered to every individual in his or her life in Christ, and has important implications for the life of the Christian community.

Where the Prayer Book provided no formal opportunity for private confession and reconciliation (primarily on account of its Roman associations), it nevertheless became the pastoral practice of the clergy in almost every place to offer it. The *Book of Alternative Services* has corrected this situation by providing two forms of the service, called "The Reconciliation of a Penitent," on pages 166–172. The introduction to the rite explains its significance as a moment of healing within the life of the church as a whole, as well as within the life of the individual who seeks it:

The Reconciliation of a Penitent, although private, is a corporate action of the Church because sin affects the unity of the Body. The absolution is restoration to full fellowship: the priest declares the forgiveness which Christ has invested in his Church. The formula

"I absolve you," which became common only in the thirteenth century, does not appear in these rites: it tends to individualize and further privatize what remains a corporate action of the Church. (*BAS* p. 166)

In other words, the absolution after confession is an act of restoration to full fellowship in the Christian community after an individual has become separated from joyful participation in it by sin. It is a moment of reconciliation between the individual and God, and the renewal of his or her baptismal innocence. The service appears immediately after the baptism and confirmation rites in order to make clear the intimate relationship between the two acts. Every baptized person needs to have opportunity for reconciliation when guilt and sinfulness have jeopardized the relationship with Christ and with other people. The absolution it provides is a new washing away of sin in the heart and conscience of the believer which restores the original baptismal purity, and assures the penitent of the grace and power of God's forgiveness.

The words of absolution emphasize this as the central purpose of the act:

Our Lord Jesus Christ, who offered himself as the perfect sacrifice to the Father, and who conferred power on his Church to forgive sins, absolve you through my ministry by the grace of the Holy Spirit, and restore you in the perfect peace of the Church. (*BAS* p. 171)

Thus, what might appear to be an essentially private moment is expressed as an extension of Christ's authority of forgiveness given to the church. The peace of Christ is offered to the penitent, whose relationships both with God and with the Christian community are healed and strengthened. This is an indication not only of the importance of incorporation, but also of the continual re-incorporation into Christ and into the fellowship of the baptized which the new rites make possible.

Saint Augustine wrote: "Thou has made us for thyself, O Lord, and our hearts are restless till they rest in thee." The social alienation which many people experience in contemporary urban life is a kind of restlessness which is rooted in a spiritual longing for fullness and for love. The new rites of the church cannot satisfy this longing. Only when the heart is turned towards God and filled with the knowledge of God's love and acceptance can the emptiness and isolation of the soul be healed. But the church can be a place where this knowledge is gained, and the worship of the church can be an event in which the soul is filled and the isolation overcome through the fact of belonging to a spiritual community, one in which God is known and celebrated with joy.

Our liturgical tradition has not prepared us well for people-making. Christendom Christianity simply assumed the community-based structure of the nation. The authors of the Prayer Book could not have foreseen the shift from community to society from their vantage point in the sixteenth century. But it has happened, and it has changed the agenda of the church's mission in the urban world. We are called to be a spiritual community in a society which promotes individualism, to affirm the dignity and worth of human beings in an economy which reduces persons to units of production, to develop supportive and nurturing relationships in the midst of competitive and consumer values. Baptism is a commitment to this new counterculture. The *Book of Alternative Services* is a set of rites for the (in this sense) anti-modern people of God.

Questions for Discussion

1. How do you feel about baptized but unconfirmed persons receiving communion?
2. What does the exchange of the peace in the eucharist mean to you?
3. How are candidates for (a) baptism, (b) confirmation, (c) marriage prepared in your church?
4. You have been invited by your rector to join a worship committee to plan the Great Easter Vigil Service. Turn to pages 321–334 in the *Book of Alternative Services.* Read the instructions carefully, noting the various options for local use. Discuss together how you would plan the service for your particular church community, specifying exactly which readings, etc., you will include. (Note: you will need an hour for this exercise.)

4.   Women and Men

It is indeed right that we should praise you,
gracious God,
for you created all things.
You formed us in your own image:
male and female you created us. . . .
You made a covenant with Israel,
and through your servants Abraham and Sarah
gave the promise of a blessing to all nations.
(from eucharistic prayer 1: *The Book of Alternative Services*)

There have been two developments in modern theology which have begun to influence North American Christianity quite substantially. One is Liberation Theology, and the other is Women's Studies in Religion. Both have introduced some important elements into the liturgies of our church.

Victors and Victims

Liberation theology has, among other things, made us aware that history has been written by the victors. The history of North America, for instance, has until very recently been written by white European immigrants. Most of the standard text books on the development of this continent start with the discovery of the eastern fishing grounds and then move on to the fur trade, which is how Europe first came to be interested in North America. One gets the impression from them that history begins at this point on the continent, and everything before it is a sort of pre-history unworthy of serious study.

Father Bill Perkins of the World Council of Churches' General Secretariat tells me that there is a satirical song going the rounds in Geneva. The words are in German, but it is a song about Columbus's first voyage to North America in 1492. As his ship approaches the coastline, Columbus sees the native people gathering on the shore. They are singing and dancing as he sails towards them. When the great navigator is close enough to pick up what they are singing, he hears the words: "We have been discovered! We have been discovered!"

Fortunately, this picture is changing. In theology, this is due in large measure to the emerging insights of the church in Latin America. For there too, history has been written by the victors. The conquistadores extended Spain's influence into the southern cone and consolidated it by a massive annihilation of the aboriginal people. Modern waves of immigration from predominantly repressive white regimes have continued this pattern of conquest and subjugation, supported by the international economy. Liberation theology has emerged in South America among the poor and their leaders, who form the vast majority of the population. It raises some serious issues for Christians throughout the world.

Theologically, it raises the question of interpretation. From whose perspective is history interpreted? The answer, say liberation thinkers, depends on your place within the social structure. The writing of history is never the mere recording of brute facts. It is always the writing of facts as seen by the person recording them. Historiography (i.e., the writing down of history) is the weighing of facts, their significance, their relationship to other facts, according to criteria of interpretation which lie outside the facts themselves. Thus, one discards details which seem unimportant to the writing of history, according to some separate criterion of significance, and highlights those which one considers essential.

The operative criterion in Latin American historiography, argue the liberationists, is the social structure itself, in short, power. Those who have power view history from the perspective of their own acquisition of it. Those who lie outside power receive no consideration. By exercising their control over the media and the organs of education, a cultural *hermeneutic* is developed among the dominant social group that sees no value in those who do not have power, or threat in those who seek to acquire it. Power thus leads to the development of a dominant world-view, a set of culturally predominant and interrelated assumptions which create the conditions of oppression for the poor and the marginalized, even though they are the majority.

What is needed, according to this argument, is a history written for and by the powerless. We need to hear from the victims in order to know the full story of a culture and its people. Powerlessness yields a very different world-view, an understanding of life and society as experienced by the oppressed. This, says liberation theology, is precisely what Christianity should provide. The Bible reveals a God who has a bias for history's victims. The biblical witness is to a God who demonstrates a preferential option for the poor, who sends his own Son to announce good news to the broken and outcast, to set captives free and cast down the mighty from their seat. But instead of articulating a world-view of the poor, Christianity has been corrupted by the rich and the strong. Theology, particularly "classical" or "Christendom" theology, has become academic and elitist. Instead of being the voice of the voiceless, it has itself adopted a dominant perspective and become a part of the world-view of the powerful. Hence, liberation theology is attempting to restate the gospel from the point of view of those to whom it was originally given.

Women and Moral Development

Women's studies also, among other things, raises the issue of whose perspective. But this time the question is asked not from the basis of class or race, but from the basis of gender. History, say many women scholars, has not only been written by the powerful, but the powerful have also been men. The dominant models of both history and Christianity are male models. They reflect the experience and attitude of only half the human race. Frequently, they argue, these attitudes and assumptions, coupled with the exercise of power, have been oppressive to women. Women's theology has therefore set out to explore the depth to which traditional Christian ideas and doctrines are based upon a gender (i.e., male)-based set of criteria and assumptions, and to reveal the extent to which this might represent an incomplete understanding of the gospel itself.

Is there a difference between male and female perspectives? Women scholars say "yes." Harvard educationalist Carol Gilligan, in an important book called *In a Different Voice*, tells the story of Jake and Amy.

These two children, both 11 years old and in the same sixth-grade class at school, participated in a study to determine whether sex-roles influence the measuring of human moral development. Gilligan describes Jake and Amy as bright and articulate, but not stereotypical of sex-roles since Amy wanted to be a scientist and Jake preferred English to math. In the study, they were each asked to respond to the following moral dilemma.

A man named Heinz must decide whether to steal in order to save the life of his wife. She has been diagnosed with a serious illness, the cure to which is an expensive drug which Heinz cannot afford. The druggist refuses to give the drug to Heinz without payment, so he must decide what to do in order to get it. Faced with this problem, Jake and Amy responded in different ways.

Jake was clear that Heinz's moral duty was to steal the drug. With unswerving logic, he constructed the dilemma as a conflict between two principles: the right to property and the right to life. Where moral principles conflict, Jake argued, there is a hierarchy of values which one must apply. Life is a higher value than property, so Heinz must steal. He was quite certain that, under the circumstances, Heinz would be acquitted of blame in any court of law.

Amy, on the other hand, felt that theft was not the answer. She was concerned that if Heinz were caught and went to jail, his wife would be even worse off. She constructed the dilemma as one of misunderstanding. The druggist could not have understood the situation. If Heinz were to take his wife to meet the druggist, she was sure the situation could be resolved. Failing that, Heinz should try to borrow the money or promise to pay the druggist back later. Amy was certain that there was another solution to the problem than the one posed in the initial explanation of the dilemma.

The conclusion Gilligan draws (in this one of many examples in the book) is that Jake and Amy see the situation from a different perspective. The boy looks at the issue with a logic based on a hierarchy of values. The girl looks at the issue with a concern for human relationships. Both agree that the life must be saved, but he resolves the problem by applying rights and responsibilities, while she resolves the problem by applying dialogue and co-operation.

In another project, Gilligan studied sex-role differences in children's games. She noted that boys tend to play competitive games, whereas girls tend to play co-operative games when both are in same-gender groups. Whenever disputes arise, she observed, boys and girls react to them differently. Boys tend to resolve disputes by appealing to the rules of the game. Failing any general agreement, the matter is usually ended by tossing a coin or taking the play over again. In girls' games, however, disputes more usually end in the termination of the game itself. This fact, noted by Kohlberg and other developmental psychologists, has usually been taken to mean that girls are less emotionally and morally mature than boys. Gilligan, however, argues that for girls relationships are more important than outcomes. Who wins is secondary to who stays friends. This is not underdevelopment, but a different perspective on values.

Gilligan's general conclusion, based on many such test projects, is that men are socialized early on in their development to construct the moral universe in terms of principles and hierarchies, while women are socialized early on to think and feel in terms of connections and relationships. If this is true, then it has important implications for our understanding of moral theology and Christian ethics, as well as raising the question of gender-bias in the scriptures themselves. At any rate, it argues for a fresh look at traditional interpretations of the gospel as they have been undertaken predominantly by men.

Convergences

There are some points of convergence here between liberation theology and women's theology. Both are critical of those aspects of the Christendom church which sought to establish and maintain itself as a powerful hierarchy in a competitive and dominating way. Both point to the oppression of the poor and women (often the same people) as essentially antithetical to true religion. Both are concerned to renew and revitalize the church by recalling us to an authentic biblical faith.

In the scriptures God is revealed as One who constantly goes out to renew relationships and to build justice. The outgoing God, whose nature is love, and who dwells in the inner relationship of Creator, Redeemer, and Sustainer, calls us to live in relationships free of oppression and the misuse of power. But as Christians we are unable to do this until we gain a radically new understanding of our own history and the class and gender biases which distort its perspectives. What is needed, the argument suggests, is a new history and theology written from the perspective of relationships rather than conquests, of co-operation rather than competition, of the victims rather than the victors. Women theologians are beginning the task, in the hope of reconstructing Christian belief into a more inclusive and holistic world-view.

Before we examine how the liturgy of the church is involved in this, let us look at the particular issue of sexuality. The church's teaching on sexuality has come under considerable scrutiny by women scholars, some of whom detect a male bias which has been oppressive to both women and men. If this is true, then we might expect a new understanding of sexuality to emerge in the language and ordering of the new rites. Since this is the case with the *Book of Alternative Services*, it is necessary to summarize the history of the church's teaching on sexuality from this new and critical perspective.

Sexuality and the Church

Jesus said little about human sexuality. Three of the gospels record a strong statement from him about the importance of sexual fidelity in marriage (see Matthew 5: 31–32, Luke 16: 18, and Mark 10: 11–12), but otherwise it seems sex was not a great concern to our Lord. It is important to note, however, that Jesus' interactions with women all demonstrate an attitude of respect and equality. Several of his disciples were women, and the first appearance of Jesus after the resurrection was to his female followers, a fact which may not be as incidental as some men think.

It is with Saint Paul, however, that specifically sexual teaching begins. The Christian community in Corinth was particularly concerned with developing a Christian understanding of sex, since the city was the centre of the cult of Aphrodite, the Greek goddess of sensual love. The temple of Aphrodite was staffed by a thousand prostitutes. Paul writes to the Corinthians primarily to explain the nature of Christian love, and to distinguish it from emotionalism, ecstasies, and the mere satisfaction of physical appetites. The wonderful description of love in 1 Corinthians 13 is still a monument to the beauty of Paul's imagination and spiritual insight.

In his letter to the Galatians, however, where he is concerned with the issue of Christian freedom, he sets forth a theory of human nature which has influenced all subsequent Christian thought and teaching about human sexuality. He posits a two-tier theory of human nature, a dualism of opposite parts which he suggests are at odds with each other in the quest for salvation. He writes:

> Walk by the Spirit, and do not gratify the desires of the flesh. For the desires of the flesh are against the Spirit, and the desires of the Spirit are against the flesh; for these are opposed to each other, to prevent you from doing what you would. . . . Now the works of the flesh are plain: immorality, impurity, licentiousness, idolatry, sorcery, enmity, strife, jealousy, anger, selfishness, dissension, party spirit, envy, drunkenness, carousing and the like. I warn you, as I warned you before, that those who do such things shall not inherit the kingdom of God. But the fruit of the Spirit is love, joy, peace, patience, kindness, goodness, faithfulness, gentleness, self-control; against such there is no law. And those who belong to Christ Jesus have crucified the flesh with its passions and desires. (Galatians 5: 16–24)

This two-tier theory of human nature suggests we have a physical and a spiritual dimension, each of which struggles against the other. Though both are aspects of our humanity, they need to be balanced against each other if we are to grow into the fullness of the stature of Christ. It is from our physical nature that evil and sinful impulses arise, whereas it is our spiritual nature that affords us the knowledge of salvation and that calls us to the higher life of holiness and purity. The evidence is strong that Paul was expressing a pastoral concern rather than a philosophical theory here. His interest appears to have been in steering the Galatians away from an overly libertarian understanding of Christian freedom, a mere indulging in wordly pleasures in the confidence of salvation in the afterlife. He was attempting to correct a misinterpretation of his teaching of the gospel by emphasizing the importance of discipline and self-control in Christian life.

Throughout his writings, Paul managed to hold together these two aspects of human nature, and never drove between them a wedge which might suggest they were utterly antithetical to each other. The responsibility for this lies with a man called Origen and, later, with Saint Augustine. Origen taught that the passions of the flesh are impure, and that those called to the higher life of grace (he distinguished between "ordinary" Christians and "perfect" souls) must sacrifice the sexual appetites in order to exemplify a Christlike devotion. Following Origen's own example of self-mutilation, young men graduating from his seminary in Alexandria were castrated as a sign of their complete commitment to Christ and the spiritual life.

Augustine took his dualism further. He had lived a life of sensual enjoyment and self-indulgence before his conversion to the Christian faith, and his relationships with women were never stable or happy. After his acceptance of Christ in his mid-thirties, Augustine began to develop a great systematic statement of Christian belief. His philosophy was based upon a theory of Being which posited a series of levels or gradations of existence from God to the lowest order of inanimate objects. Natural to this system was the idea of higher and lower natures, and Augustine taught that men and women were composed of both of these, the higher nature consisting of the faculty of reason and the lower nature consisting of the physical appetites, such as the sex drive.

It is through the exercise of the higher faculties of reason and understanding, Augustine argued, that people come to the knowledge of God. Sexuality was necessary in the divine order of creation but merely for the continuation of the species. At its worst it posed a threat to human salvation by opening the door to satanic temptations. It was through the act of sexual intercourse, he suggested, that the taint of Original Sin was passed from generation to generation. We inherit the Fall of Adam by the act of procreation. The redeemed life, on the other hand, leads to the renunciation of these desires and temptations, and issues in a commitment to sexual abstention and the subjugation of physical appetites other than the ones necessary for survival. This has created the tradition that human sexuality is essentially sinful.

Augustine's influence on Western Christianity, and therefore on our liturgy, has been immense. It extends all the way from fifth-century North Africa to sixteenth-century England. The service of Publick Baptism in the 1662 edition of the Prayer Book, for example, begins with the words:

Dearly beloved, forasmuch as all men are conceived and born in sin, (and that which is born of the flesh is flesh,) and they that are in the flesh cannot please God, but live in sin, committing many actual transgressions . . . .

So pervasive is his influence that it is almost impossible for contemporary men and women to go back beyond his teaching on sexuality and read the New Testament in a different way. By the early Middle Ages, the Pauline balance had given way to a marked antithesis in the duality of human nature. The wholeness and complementarity of the spiritual and physical aspects of human nature was abandoned, and in its place there arose a body of theory and teaching about sexuality which had four historic consequences for Western culture.

Four Consequences of Spirit/Flesh Dualism

1. *Love became separated from sex.* After Origen and Augustine, official church attitudes to sexuality began to differentiate the sex act from acts of love. It was felt that the activity of sexual intercourse belonged to our lower or "base" self, and love as a dimension of the spiritual or higher self. It was emphasized, of course, that the birth of our Lord had involved no act of intercourse, and that Jesus himself had never married. Pure love, therefore, became associated with the renunciation of sex, and sex itself was relegated to the level of a purely necessary, but not necessarily pure, function of the human body.

By the Middle Ages, this dualism ushered in the era of courtly love. The age of chivalry and aristocratic romance was built upon the separation of love and sex. Since pure love was understood to be non-sexual, the romantic ideal became the relationship of unrequited passion. The literature of the period depicts knights in shining armour engaging in acts of noble sacrifice and derring-do all for the sake of a maiden's smile. The love of the noble knight for the damsel in distress was never requited or satisfied sexually, for this would tarnish the code of honour that bound these doyens of chivalry together. In fact, the practice among the mediaeval (male) aristocracy was to take a wife for the purposes of childbearing, but to reserve one's love for another woman outside marriage. For women this meant making the choice between being married and being loved. Marriage for love was for the peasants.

The Prayer Book captures this ideal in a marvellously revealing passage. The 1662 edition of the Marriage Service contains this purple prose:

> [Marriage is] not by any to be enterprised, nor taken in hand, unadvisedly, lightly, or wantonly, to satisfy men's carnal lusts and appetites, like brute beasts that have no understanding; but reverently, discreetly, advisedly, soberly, and in the fear of God; duly considering the causes for which matrimony was ordained.
>
> First, it was ordained for the procreation of children, to be brought up in the fear and nurture of the Lord, and to the praise of his holy Name.
>
> Secondly, it was ordained for a remedy against sin, and to avoid fornication; that such persons as have not the gift of continency might marry, and keep themselves undefiled members of Christ's body.

This is hardly a "high" view of matrimony! The Augustinian heritage bequeathed an attitude to marriage of grudging tolerance. It was considered second-best to a relationship of pure and total devotion to God, and the church saw its purpose as primarily for procreation and secondly as a means of discouraging fornication. The Canadian revision of 1962 introduced fundamental changes to this understanding, which, as we shall see, are continued in the *Book of Alternative Services*.

2. *Men and women were differentiated according to higher/lower natures.* It was a short step from the intellectual separation of love and sex to the social separation of male and female roles in the mediaeval world. The presumption was made that men were by divine intention called to things of a higher nature. Government, business, education, and the pursuit of reason were considered their proper vocation. Women, on the other hand, were deemed to belong to the baser realm of physical appetites, earthiness, and fertility.

Menstruation myths encouraged women to see themselves as belonging to a lower order. Their proper vocation was to childbearing and the domestic duties. Women were socialized in the early Middle Ages away from intellectual and public life into roles of domesticity and family nurture. Men were socialized away from childraising and into roles of economic importance.

After the Industrial Revolution in the nineteenth century, women assumed increasing economic value as sources of cheap and exploitable labour. Social attitudes towards women changed as it became obvious they might have a use for men outside the home. Women entered the workplace, and it was not long after that they began to realize this had given them a certain political leverage to press for changes in their limited social and economic roles. The first serious attempt by women to gain equality with men came with the movement for universal suffrage; the right to vote. But when this burst upon the world of men in the early part of this century, the old arguments of differentiation between higher and lower natures surfaced again. The church was in the forefront of the battle to maintain a traditional "Christian" separation between men and women. An interview with American Cardinal Gibbons at the time of the suffrage movement illustrates the point:

> "Women suffrage?" questioned the cardinal . . . . "I am surprised that anyone should ask the question. I have but one answer to such a question, and that is that I am unalterably opposed to women's suffrage, always have been, and always will be. . . . Why should a woman lower herself to sordid politics? Why should a woman leave her home and go into the street to play the game of politics? Why should she long to come into contact with men at the polling places? Why should she long to rub elbows with men who are her inferiors intellectually and morally? Why should a woman long to go into the streets and leave behind her happy home, her children, a husband and everything that goes to make up ideal domestic life? . . . When a woman enters the political arena she goes outside the sphere for which she was intended. She gains nothing by that journey. On the other hand, she loses the exclusiveness, respect, and dignity to which she is entitled in her home.
>
> Who wants to see a woman standing around the polling places; speaking to a crowd on the street corner; pleading with those in attendance at a political meeting? Certainly such a sight would not be relished by her husband or by her children. Must the child,

returning from school, go to the polls to find his mother? Must the husband, returning from work, go to the polls to find his wife soliciting votes from this man or that? . . . Woman is queen," said the cardinal in bringing the interview to a close, "but her kingdom is the domestic kingdom." (Quoted in *From Machismo to Mutuality* by Rosemary Reuther and Eugene Bianchi)

The cardinal was actually reversing the traditional higher/lower order of roles in order to support his distaste for female politicians, raising women above men in the divine scheme of things, no doubt thinking himself very modern and enlightened. But this "idealisation of woman" (Reuther's term), which has been a feature of Western dualism, has the same effect of separating women from public life by placing them on a pedestal above it. The impact on women is the same as if they are regarded as inferior.

3. *Virginity was elevated to the level of a spiritual virtue.* After purity had become equated with sexual innocence in church teaching, and the highest forms of love were divorced from human sexuality, the most devout expressions of the religious life became associated with virginity and chastity. This was the case for both men and women. Anyone who wished to serve God in the most virtuous possible way was directed to seek the monastic or cloistered life, where vows of sexual abstinence were mandatory. The monastic movement, from the time of the "desert fathers" in the early years of the Constantinian era to the Rule of Saint Benedict, institutionalized the principle of separation between sexuality and spirituality. (Benedict once threw himself into a thicket of brambles after he felt desire for a passing girl.) The effect of this still manifests itself today in a suspicion of sexuality among those who seek a deeper knowledge of God — as well as in the sometimes reckless sexual abandon of those who see no spiritual dimension to the act.

Sometime during the Middle Ages, the cult of virginity became popularized in the widespread devotion to the Blessed Virgin Mary. This had not been a feature of the apostolic or pre-Constantinian church, where Mary was certainly honoured, but not worshipped. The age of courtly love led naturally to the veneration of our Lord's mother, since she symbolized all the virtues of so-called "true womanhood" (Reuther) as they appeared to men. She had been chaste, submissive, and obedient, according to the infancy narratives in two of the gospels, and the cult of her adoration served to remind women that they should strive to be like her. For men, she served as the most perfect object of unrequitable devotion, a supreme expression of the purity of love in its captivity to sexual innocence. All who wished to attain the heights of spiritual perfection needed only to gaze upon the face of our Lady and abandon all thought of physical pleasure. This is the beginning of the idealisation process which led to the cardinal's dismay.

In fact, the gospels indicate that Mary was chosen by God to be the mother of the world's Saviour not so much because she was chaste, but because she was of low estate. The Magnificat, which has a rich and time-honoured place in Anglican evening worship, celebrates the fact that, by gifting Mary with this birth, God had raised up the humble and meek and put down the mighty from their seat, sending the rich empty away and scattering the proud in the imagination of their hearts. It is a song of exaltation at God's mercy to the lowly (rather than the virginal) and reveals Mary's own understanding of the political significance of the event. She saw herself as participating in the overturning of the prevailing social order.

The Virgin Birth does not play a central role in the New Testament itself. It came to enjoy a place of prominence in Christianity only after Origen and Augustine. Only two of the Gospels record the fact at all (Matthew and Luke), and then the matter is dropped by them and never mentioned again after the opening chapters. The other two gospels, Mark (the earliest) and John (the latest), never allude directly or indirectly to it, and the letters of Paul, which pre-date most of the gospels, betray no knowledge of a unique birth.

Paul, in fact, makes mention of the birth of Jesus only to show that it was in every way ordinary: "born of a woman, born under the law" (Galatians 4: 4). He appears to be suggesting that Jesus was born in similar circumstances to us in order to enter fully into human flesh so as to redeem it. Whatever the meaning, he seems to be unaware of any miraculous conception, and it played no part in his preaching and teaching. The accumulation of this evidence, therefore, suggests that the Virgin Birth arose as a belief sometime during the course of the first century, after the resurrection and after Paul, and gained ground in the piety of the church only after the theology of Augustine laid the ground for its further development.

Devotion to the Virgin Mary has always had a place in Anglican worship, but it has never played a central role in Anglican spirituality (except perhaps in Anglo-Catholic circles, where it receives a balanced and not obsessive emphasis). The Prayer Book contains a set of propers (i.e., collect, epistle, and gospel) for the Purification of Saint Mary the Virgin (BCP p. 266–7), for the Annunciation (p. 271), and for the Commemoration of the Blessed Virgin Mary (p. 309) since these all appear on the church's calendar of the liturgical year. In general, however, she has recovered her pre-Constantinian place of veneration but not worship in our tradition, and Anglicans have not recognized the specifically Marian doctrines of the Roman Catholic church — namely, the Immaculate Conception and the Assumption — as normative for faith.

4. *Celibacy was imposed upon the clergy.* For the first thousand years of the church's history, the marriage of clergy was quite common. In the Eastern (later Orthodox) tradition, married men could be admitted to the orders of deacon and priest provided matrimony preceded ordination. Bishops were to remain celibate, but this was because the Eastern church chose its bishops from among its monks who had already sworn this vow. In the Orthodox tradition, this remains the practice today.

In the West, however, various attempts were made in the centuries after Augustine to impose celibacy on all clergy. As the view developed that marriage was a second-best vocation, and the ideal of non-sexual love gained ascendancy in spiritual teaching, it was felt that those making the profession of orders in the parishes as well as in the monasteries should embrace the discipline of continency or sexual abstinence. The Second Lateran Council of 1139 made the marriage of clergy unlawful and, further, rendered the unions of those clergy married at the time invalid. From that day to this, the practice of forced celibacy remains the norm for Roman Catholic clergy.

The Anglican church, however, broke with this position soon after its beginning. Article 32 of the Articles of Religion states:

Bishops, priests, and deacons are not commanded by God's Law, either to vow the estate of single life, or to abstain from marriage: therefore it is lawful for them, as for all other Christian men, to marry at their own discretion, as they shall judge the same to serve better to godliness.
(*BCP* p. 711)

This enactment technically legalized the marriage of Thomas Cranmer, the Archbishop of Canterbury! But it was also a triumph for English moderation and common sense. Though it was never spoken of in these words, there was an implicit recognition from the start that clergy are sexual beings and share all the normal impulses of human nature. Even the Prayer Book's low view of marriage did not blind the architects of Anglicanism to the basic facts of life.

The official reason for the acceptance of clerical marriage, however, was theological. There is no scriptural basis for forced celibacy. Though our Lord was not married, he never forbade the practice among his disciples. Even Saint Paul — who was not the misogynist he is often made out to be — felt that "it is better to marry than to burn" (1 Corinthians 7: 9). The influence of Protestant theology on the English church at the time of the break with Rome brought a new consciousness of the authority of scripture into the minds of the clergy and people, and whatever was not expressly forbidden in the Bible was deemed to be a matter for personal discretion. This had been the position taken by Martin Luther on the continent, who sealed his own break with Rome by marrying a nun.

Voluntary celibacy, on the other hand, is and always has been a part of the personal discretion exercised by Anglicans, clergy and laity alike. It is accorded a proper respect by our church when it is chosen as a spiritual discipline by either men or women, and it has never been imposed. Celibacy in our tradition has not been interpreted as a discipline superior to marriage. When it is experienced as a personal vocation, rather than required as an ecclesiastical expectation, it is not tied to a necessarily anti-sexual theology, and therefore takes on a genuine quality of virtue which may be appropriate to the circumstances of particular persons.

Anglicanism, therefore, has historically resisted some of the more extreme conclusions of the Christendom church's attitudes to human sexuality. Nevertheless, it has been strongly influenced by the spirit/flesh dualism of Augustine and has incorporated many aspects of it into the liturgy. Women's theology has made a great contribution to our understanding of liturgy and spirituality by uncovering this history of teaching about sexuality, and by pointing out the places where it has been oppressive to women.

The changing role of women in post-Christendom society has brought a new awareness of history among scholars, and a new search for mutuality between women and men among a great many Christians. Oppressive roles and structures are destructive of true Christian community, and diminish the full dignity of both women and men. The task of reconstructing Christian belief in pursuit of a liberating mutuality is now well under way, and will be a feature of theological and liturgical revision for many years to come. Some of the fruit of this work is beginning to be reflected in the new services, and the *Book of Alternative Services* has made a tentative start in incorporating some of the insights of women's theology into Anglican worship. Let us examine four areas in the new rites which reveal a new sensitivity to the intrinsic equality of women and men.

The Marriage Service

The Prayer Book wedding ceremony, before its revision in Canada in 1962, not only expressed a mediaeval view of sex ("like brute beasts that have no understanding") but also entrenched in marriage an oppressive dualism of sex roles. It reflected an era when women were expected to be secondary to and dependent upon men. Bride and groom were each required to make different vows, as befitted their different roles. The man was to promise to love, comfort, honour, and keep his wife, while the woman was to promise to love, comfort, honour, and obey her husband. Thus, the church assigned a particular place to both partners in the relationship, and established a clear hierarchy of authority in the home.

Interestingly enough, matrimony has not always been regarded by the church as a sacrament. For the first thousand years of Christian history, it was more usual to enter it in a secular ceremony outside the church, and it was only in the eleventh century that Holy Matrimony as such was taken into the rites and ceremonies of Christianity. When this happened, the Christian model of marriage was borrowed from the political model of the state. Just as the state was governed and held together by a hierarchy of authority, consisting of a monarch, aristocracy, and serfs in descending order, so too the Christian home was to have a head and a descending order of leadership.

The headship was naturally given to the man, and the woman was given the place of man's companion. Later rulings of the church gave the husband the legal rite to chastise and beat his wife if she failed in her vows of obedience to him. (This is the origin of the term *rule of thumb*. A man was allowed to strike his wife with a stick no wider than his thumb.) Support for this ordering of the roles in marriage was claimed from the New Testament and from the letters of both Peter and Paul. They too, of course, had taken over a patriarchal model of marriage from their Jewish ancestry. Thus is was accorded the status of "divine ordinance" by the church, much as the ordering of the state itself was felt, for a time, to be inviolable and sacred.

Furthermore, the Prayer Book wedding service was principally a contract between two men. The bride's father brought the woman into the church and handed her over to the groom. There is a rubric in the liturgy which directs the father to give the bride's hand to the minister, who then places it into the groom's hand (see page 566 in the 1962 edition). The symbolism of this is transparent. The deeds to the property are being handed over! Though it could not, of course, take place without the woman's consent, the whole transaction was designed to reinforce the belief that women are chattels, and must at all times be owned by men. No one brought the groom into church, or was asked "who giveth this man to be married to this woman?" The Prayer Book treats men as free agents, while women must be given away.

The *Book of Alternative Services*, on the other hand, expresses a fundamentally different doctrine of marriage. It contains a statement about the mutuality of love between husband and wife, and points to the importance of equality of responsibility in the Christian home. No particular sex roles are imposed by the rite — if traditional roles are chosen by the couple, this is quite a different matter — but instead the partnership of marriage is stressed, as well as the accountability of one to the other and both to God. The vows each partner is required to make are the same. Both must promise to love, comfort, honour, and keep. Neither has to obey. Is the model here perhaps that of a republic rather than a monarchy? Whatever it may be, the new service captures a more balanced approach to marriage roles, and is a significant step away from the earlier dualism.

Whereas the Prayer Book rite in its 1662 form regarded marriage as a remedy for lust, the new liturgy celebrates it as a means of grace, a blessing of God, and a sign of the unity between Christ and the church:

Marriage is a gift of God and a means of his grace, in which man and woman become one flesh. It is God's purpose that, as husband and wife give themselves to each other in love, they shall grow together and be united in that love, as Christ is united with his Church.

The union of man and woman in heart, body, and mind is intended for their mutual comfort and help, that they may know each other with delight and tenderness in acts of love [and that they may be blessed in the procreation, care, and upbringing of children].
(*BAS* p. 541)

Here, love-making is celebrated rather than despised, and sex is no longer limited to procreation but presented as a natural expression of tenderness and love between married partners — which may or may not issue in children (this is the significance of the bracketed statement) as the individual circumstances of the couple dictate.

Further, the new rite sets marriage in the context of the wider human community. It is not a private family event, but a relationship which takes place in a network of surrounding relationships and points the couple outward into the world and to their responsibilities as baptized members of Christ. Where the old rite involved only the bride, the groom, and the bride's father in the action of the liturgy, the *Book of Alternative Services* requires the guests and friends of the couple present at the ceremony to pledge their support and encouragement to them during the years to come (see p. 544). And where, formerly, only the father of the bride was asked for his consent to the proceedings, in the new rite the celebrant asks all members of both families:

Celebrant   Do you, members of the families of *N* and *N*, give your blessing to this marriage?

And they answer "We do." This change in the service serves to ground the marriage in a context of supportive and encouraging relationships, involving both the in-laws and the Christian family as responsible participants in the sacrament. In this way, family life is incorporated into the purpose of the caring community, and women and men are reminded not only of their fellowship with each other but also with others outside the home. Marriage, in the *Book of Alternative Services*, is another act of people-making.

Inclusive Language

Language is the vehicle of meaning. It is through the medium of human language that we construct and communicate our perceptions of reality. Modern linguistic philosophy has explored the relationship between language and knowledge in exhaustive detail, concluding that the two are inseparable in both theory and practice. What cannot be spoken of, cannot be known. At the same time, there is an unavoidable necessity to put into language what is known, and to create new language to express new knowledge when that cannot be contained within the limits of the language we already possess. As our perceptions change, therefore, so must the words we use.

The Prayer Book is quite authentic in its reflection of the cultural assumptions about male/female relations in Reformation England. The Canadian revision of 1962 made no changes to these assumptions. The word *men* was considered to include the whole of the human race, and *he* meant *she* as well. In the last 25 years, however, many women have come to feel excluded rather than included by these terms. As women have gained a deeper understanding of the male-oriented structure of society, so many have come to see how this is supported and affirmed by the male-oriented structure of language.

In 1980, the General Synod of the Anglican church of Canada passed this motion:

> That this Synod recommends to the Doctrine and Worship Committee that in any revision of liturgy, due care be taken to use inclusive language wherever possible. (Act 25)

The *Book of Alternative Services* attempts to do this by adopting more inclusive words when speaking of women and men together. This does *not* mean substituting female terms for male terms. There is no suggestion, for example, of replacing "Our Father who art in heaven" with "Our Mother." The solution to the dilemma of how to incorporate changing perceptions is not to create sexism in reverse. This is made clear in a pamphlet published in 1983 by the Participation Task Force of the National Women's Unit of the Anglican Church. Called *Guidelines for Inclusive Language*, the pamphlet sets out an agenda for the use of words and phrases that include both sexes without jarring alterations to liturgical or scriptural texts.

Some of the recommendations of the Task Force have been followed by the *Book of Alternative Services*, as the table below may illustrate:

Exclusive	*Inclusive*
It is right to give him thanks and praise. (Third Canadian Eucharist)	It is right to give our thanks and praise (*BAS* Great Thanksgiving)
He who comes to me will never be hungry. (Third Canadian Eucharist)	Whoever comes to me will never be hungry. (*BAS* Sentence at the Fraction)
For in thy sight shall no man living be justified. (*BCP* Psalm 143)	For in your sight shall no one living be justified. (*BAS* Psalm 143)
honourable among all men. (*BCP* Marriage Service)	a way of life that all should reverence. (*BAS* Celebration and Blessing of a Marriage)
If any man sin, we have an Advocate. (*BCP* Comfortable Words)	If anyone sin, we have an Advocate. *BAS* — re-ordered *BCP* rite)
Maker of all things, Judge of all men. (*BCP* Eucharist)	Maker of all things, judge of all people. (*BAS* Eucharist)
a true saying, worthy of all men to be received. (*BCP* Comfortable Words)	a true saying, worthy of all to be received. (*BAS* — re-ordered *BCP* rite)
in earth peace, good will towards men. (*BCP* Gloria)	And peace to his people on earth. (*BAS* Gloria)
and manfully to fight under his banner. (*BCP* Baptism Service)	Omitted altogether in the *BAS*.

The assumption in the new rites is that the word *men* is not generic and does not adequately express the fullness of male and female community. Gender-limited phrases are not inclusive. These changes in phrase are simple enough and quite within the bounds of literary taste. Most of them, in fact, are barely noticeable. Yet they indicate a commitment in the church to the shaping of a new community between women and men in post-Christendom society.

The broadening of language in the new rites is intended to have the effect of raising the awareness of Anglicans to the importance of inclusion, and in time may help to bring changes in the participation of women in the leadership and councils of the church, which was a commitment made by the General Synod of 1980. It is hoped that clergy and lay leaders will incorporate inclusive language into other aspects of the liturgy as well, such as sermons and intercessions and music, wherever possible.

Sexual Stereotyping

The *Guidelines for Inclusive Language* of 1983 state:

Men and women should be treated primarily as people, and not primarily as members of the opposite sexes. Their shared humanity and common attributes should be stressed — not their gender differences. Neither sex should be stereotyped or arbitrarily assigned to a leading or secondary role. . . . Characteristics that have been traditionally praised in males — such as boldness, initiative, and assertiveness — should also be praised in females. Characteristics that have been praised in females — such as gentleness, compassion, and sensitivity — should also be praised in males.

The Christendom language of the church tended to present men as natural leaders. They were shown as independent, strong, and decisive. Women, on the other hand, were often presented as naturally humble, meek, submissive, and dependent. The *Book of Alternative Services* attempts to avoid this stereotypical falsehood in a number of ways.

First, it avoids the assumption that clergy and church leaders are all male. The ordination of women to the priesthood in 1976 in

Canada makes it no longer appropriate to refer to the celebrant or minister in the liturgy as *he*. The rubrics in the new rites are adjusted accordingly. Where the Prayer Book could quite accurately speak of the *clergyman* and the priest or minister as *he*, the *Book of Alternative Services* simply changes this to the *celebrant* and omits both male and female pronouns when referring to celebrants, lay or ordained.

Secondly, it avoids the assumption that all laity are male. The Prayer Book rubrics give occasional direction to *laymen* to do this or that, and refer to members of the congregation as though they were all men. The *Book of Alternative Services* uses the simple device of saying "a member of the congregation shall. . . " or " a layperson shall. . . ."

Third, it avoids the linguistic equation of men with all human beings, as though one sex were representative of both. Examples of this are listed above, but further instances include use of the term *children of God* instead of *sons of God* and a much more frequent use of *people of God*.

Fourth, it omits references to manliness and masculinity when attempting to express the nature of Christian life and the qualities of Christian character. Perhaps the clearest piece of stereotyping in the Prayer Book is the exhortation during the baptism service "manfully to fight under his banner against sin, the world, and the devil; and to continue Christ's faithful soldier and servant unto his life's end." We might ask why it is "manful" to fight. The destruction of two world wars in this century, along with the imminent danger of nuclear holocaust, has made modern liturgists more careful about the use of militaristic images and exhortations to aggression.

In early church, the profession of soldier was considered to the immoral for baptized Christians, and those coming into the church were asked to take up a more peaceful life. In the modern church, the commitment to peace-making is expressed in the liturgy not only by direct statements about it in connection with mission, but also in the avoidance of imagery of combat and references to the church as a "mighty army" and so on. The new baptism service has dropped the fighting language, with its sexist tones, and uses instead the imagery of service and struggle. Thus:

Celebrant	Will you persevere in resisting evil and, whenever you fall into sin, repent and return to the Lord?
People	I will, with God's help.
Celebrant	Will you seek and serve Christ in all persons, loving your neighbour as yourself?
People	I will, with God's help.
Celebrant	Will you strive for justice amd peace among all people, and respect the dignity of every human being?
People	I will, with God's help.
	(*BAS* p. 159)

There is no lessening of Christian determination or commitment here. But there is an absence of triumphalism and of linking faithfulness with manliness. Perseverance, resistance to evil, love, and respect are universal human qualities which men and women share equally.

The Femininity of God

All human language falls short of the reality of God. Christian theology has never imagined it could offer an exhaustive and complete definition of God in any of its doctrines and creeds. In fact, the most careful attempts to say anything at all about the "ultimate Reality with which we have to do" (Gordon Kaufman) have always been couched in careful disclaimers about the inadequacy of finite words and concepts. In the language of scholastic theology, God is beyond number and gender. God is to be understood in terms of *aseity* — that is, uniquely in and of itself (Latin *a se, "unto itself"*). Masculine and feminine gender are therefore both inaccurate attributes of the supreme God.

However, we have to say something about God or remain silent altogether. We must try to "eff the ineffable," as a colleague of mine says. The difficulty posed by the English language, unlike some others, is that it possesses no personal pronoun in neuter. The impersonal *it* is clearly unsatisfactory to express the personal God who loves us and gives up his (!) life for us.(One has difficulty even imagining how to write that sentence in a different way in English.) Earlier centuries, however, content to allow masculine terminology to be applied to God as well as to humanity, have bequeathed us a heritage of gender-biased language about the attributes of God. The impression is easily gained that God is male. This is now perceived as part of the oppressive structure of language by many women, and as inaccurate theology by scholars (of both sexes).

The 1983 *Guidelines* address this problem helpfully:

> All descriptions of divinity are analogical. The weight of traditional analogy has been on the male side of the balance, but not exclusively. Care should be taken to redress the balance, not by eradicating traditional paternal imagery, nor by substituting exclusive maternal imagery in its place, but by expanding the range of feminine symbols as well as symbols which retain the personal insight of Christianity but avoid sexual bias. (p. 27)

The *Book of Alternative Services* expands the limited male imagery of both the *Book of Common Prayer* and the Third Canadian Eucharist by incorporating some broader symbols and attributes into the language of liturgy. Feminine attributes expressing nurture, compassion, gentleness, and life-giving nature — which have always been part of the Christian understanding of God, but have not played a central role in liturgical imagery — are now applied to the language of praise and worship. Instead of the rather heavy traditional emphasis on God as "eternal Father, mighty King, dreadful Judge," etc., we have in the new rites some rather exciting new forms of address:

God for whom we wait
(*BAS* p. 269)

Faithful God
(*BAS* p. 270)

God of hope, merciful God
(*BAS* p. 271)

Gracious God
(*BAS* p. 272)

The Answer

Lowell Fillmore

When for a purpose
I had prayed and prayed and prayed
Until my words seemed worn and bare
   With arduous use,
And I had knocked and asked and
   knocked and asked again,
And all my fervor and persistence
   brought no hope,
I paused to give my weary brain a rest
And ceased my anxious human cry.
   In that still moment,
After self had tried and failed,
There came a glorious vision of God's
   power,
And, lo, my prayer was answered in
   that hour.

UNITY SCHOOL OF CHRISTIANITY, UNITY VILLAGE, MO 64065

Printed U.S.A. 310   C-14-6659-5M-3-88 C

To: Molly & Darnley

Love & Blessings

Source of light and gladness
Generous Creator
God of peace, God of light
Source of truth and joy
God of power and life
(*BAS* pp. 273–278)

These phrases move away from misleading attributions of specific gender to God, and point to other, less masculine, characteristics which are equally part of our experience of God. The new liturgies attempt to capture a fuller and more comprehensive imagery which will hopefully allow those men and women who find the old language painful and an obstacle to full participation in worship to have a respected place within the Christian community again.

It must be said, however that the *Book of Alternative Services* has a long way to go yet in the reconstruction of liturgical language. Masculine pronouns still abound throughout its pages, and it is unlikely to satisfy any but the most moderate of critics. Nevertheless, a book of worship may not run too far ahead of the church, and it can only be hoped (I express a personal opinion, of course) that future revisions will bring more daring changes.

Dominican priest Matthew Fox, modern founder of the school of creation spirituality, argues in his book *Original Blessing* that Western Christianity since Augustine has been unable to free itself from its powerful Fall/Redemption model of religious belief. Augustine saw the Fall as the central paradigm of the human situation, and sin as the perpetual condition of the human body from which Christ came to save us. This, Fox points out, is an interpretation of the scriptures open to dispute. It would be equally possible to take God's act of creation as the central paradigm of faith, and to interpret the coming of Christ as Saviour as the fulfilment of God's creativity and love, and thus to understand history and nature (including the human body) as intrinsically good and as the *locus* of salvation.

Fox may not win the day against Augustine, but he does show that the Western spiritual tradition has created an antithesis between sexuality and spirituality which has been not altogether helpful to the goal of human wholeness or redemption. Both our sexuality and our spirituality are united by *eros* — the creative life force, the impulse toward union and harmony with God and with others. Eros drives us towards one another and towards the Creator, but it is irrational and uncontrollable, a potent and sometimes devastating force which can lead in unpredictable directions. The church has been suspicious of eros, and has sought to transform it into *agape*, a non-sensual, almost intellectual, form of love, devoid of passion. But eros is a gift of God too, and needs to be recovered in a healthy Christian spirituality.

Women, so long the victims of anti-erotic suspicion, have now begun to find some liberation from the past and to make a new important contribution to spirituality in the church. This is just beginning to make itself felt in the liturgy. The attempt by the *Book of Alternative Services* to create a new harmony between women and men in the form of the new marriage service is an encouraging development. The tentative and uncertain efforts to develop a new language and imagery of God is to be commended. But these efforts need to go much further if a mutuality of the sexes within the church is to be enhanced.

Questions for Discussion

1. Does religious language seem sexist to you? How do you react to male imagery when it is attributed to God?
2. Do you feel that human sexuality is part of a lower nature in us? What will you say to St. Paul when you see him?
3. What does the term *femininity of God* mean to you?
4. Read the following extract from the 1662 Marriage Service and then look at pages 528–529 in the *Book of Alternative Services*. In what ways do these documents differ in their understanding of:

   — the relation between love and sex?
   — the roles of women and men in the family?
   — the purpose of God in ordaining marriage?

From the Solemnization of Matrimony (1662)

   Dearly beloved, we are gathered together here in the sight of God, and in the face of this congregation, to join together this Man and this Woman in holy Matrimony; which is an honourable estate, instituted of God in the time of man's innocency, signifying unto us the mystical union that is betwixt Christ and his Church; which holy estate Christ adorned and beautified with his presence, and first miracle that he wrought, in Cana of Galilee; and is commended of Saint Paul to be honourable among all men: and therefore is not by any to be enterprised, nor taken in hand, unadvisedly, lightly, or wantonly, to satisfy men's carnal lusts and appetites, like brute beasts that have no understanding; but reverently, discreetly, advisedly, soberly, and in the fear of God; duly considering the causes for which Matrimony was ordained.

First, It was ordained for the procreation of children, to be brought up in the fear and nurture of the Lord, and to the praise of his holy Name.

Secondly, It was ordained for a remedy against sin, and to avoid fornication; that such persons as have not the gift of continency might marry, and keep themselves undefiled members of Christ's body.

Thirdly, It was ordained for the mutual society, help, and comfort, that the one ought to have of the other, both in prosperity and adversity. Into which holy estate these two persons present come now to be joined. Therefore if any man can show any just cause, why they may not lawfully be joined together, let him now speak, or else hereafter for ever hold his peace.

5. Spirituality

Almighty God,
you have made us for yourself,
and our hearts are restless
until they find their rest in you.
May we find peace in your service,
and in the world to come, see you face to face.
(A prayer of St. Augustine: *BAS* p. 367)

By spirituality I mean our relationship with God. Like all relationships, this is a complex and in the end indefinable thing. God, like people, is ultimately beyond our ability to comprehend, and it is a rare person who understands what his or her relationship with God will bring today, much less tomorrow. The essential thing about relationships is that they will always remain mysterious and impenetrable to our minds. And they constantly grow and change. Human spirituality is the most mysterious and impenetrable of all, and the most transforming, for it is about our relationship with the ultimate and glorious Mystery at the heart of creation, which contains and sustains life itself.

My hope in this chapter is not to offer any final statement on human spirituality as a whole, or to unfold the vast enterprise which is the soul's journey back to God. It is simply to explore how liturgy is a part of this journey, and how our tradition of worship in the Anglican church has shaped and formed our relationship with God. To begin, let us understand something about ourselves and our tradition.

Three Types of Church Tradition

Among the variety of Christian denominations can be discerned three broad types: (a) experiential, (b) confessional, and (c) liturgical. Though each may contain elements of the other, in most denominations one or other of these types prevails as the dominant characteristic.

1. Experiential. The experiential tradition emphasizes the importance of seeking a personal relationship with God. Churches of this type encourage strong emotional experiences of the power of God in individual lives, an identifiable moment of religious awakening which is followed by a palpable and visible transformation of life. A well-known example of such an experience is that of Anglican evangelist John Wesley. On the evening of 24 May 1738, according to his own diary, "I went very unwillingly to a society in Aldersgate Street, where one was reading Luther's preface to the Epistle to the Romans. About a quarter before nine, while he was describing the change which God works in the heart through faith in Christ, I felt my heart strangely warmed. I felt I did trust in Christ, Christ alone, for my salvation; and an assurance was given me that he had taken my sins away, even mine, and saved me from the law of sin and death."

Wesley's life was altered from that moment on, and his subsequent ministry was an attempt to bring the same experience to others. People of the evangelical tradition, both within and outside the Anglican church, regard this sort of personal transformation as the defining characteristic of Christian life, the authentic sign of belonging to Christ, and gear all their liturgy and ministry to inducing the experience as widely as possible. Preaching, for instance, whether in church or on the street corner is frequently of the testimonial kind, aimed at gaining the conversion of the hearers. Hymns and prayers call upon the individual to open up the heart and stress the importance of personal salvation.

Within the larger Anglican tradition, this experientialism has provided a healthy counterbalance to the often cerebral nature of our worship and spirituality. It has usually surfaced after periods of spiritual dullness in the church, when faith has lost its vitality and excitement and has descended into a dry intellectualism or merely empty ritual. When divorced from the corporate life of the wider church, however, it has frequently descended to a sort of experience - fundamentalism. To be a Christian you must have had a religious ecstasy, and you are not a Christian if you haven't. This narrow focus leads to a self-centred and individualistic spirituality.

It is exclusive and elitist in its grasp of the gospel, and tends to disintegrate into even more exclusive and even more elitist sects each claiming to be truly saved. It is hardly surprising that churches of this type are adamantly opposed to ecumenism.

2. Confessional. The confessional tradition includes those churches which have produced statements of doctrine or belief, which the individual must be able to confess in order to be received as a member. The emphasis here is not so much on emotional experience as on intellectual assent. In response to the question "What must I believe in order to follow Jesus Christ?" the churches of this type answer: "Accept and agree to the following truths. . . ." The Presbyterian church is an example of a confessional church. Its Westminster Confession still serves, at least nominally, as a basis for teaching, and provides a norm for the instruction of new believers and inquirers. The Roman Catholic church also has a strong confessional basis. It has a long history of issuing normative statements of teaching in the form of papal bulls, edicts, and articles of faith to which members of that church are required to subscribe.

The issuance of definitive statements about Christian belief is a response to the natural human desire for clarity and understanding in religion. It is also a response to attacks on Christianity from without or within. The apostolic church found it necessary to distinguish the new faith from its Jewish roots. In later centuries, the church summoned great councils in various attempts to combat heresy and define orthodoxy, producing such statements of belief as the Nicene Creed. The Reformation was another period of defining and distinguishing in which both Catholic and Protestant traditions attempted to state their differing views of the gospel.

The value in these exercises is that they bring a critical reason to bear on matters of faith. Whereas the religion of the heart may provide emotional satisfaction, the confessional approach recognizes the importance of understanding, and brings faith out of the necessarily private domain of individual feelings into the public domain of discussion and clarification. At the same time, the danger in this tradition is of an overly intellectual or rational spirituality. Dogmatism, which is the attempt to fit God into a doctrinal box and then force people into it, is a recurrent problem in traditions which have a strong intellectual depth. It tends to provoke the opposite reaction, such as the outbreak of the Charismatic Movement in mainstream churches after a somewhat rationalistic and spiritually barren period during the last years of Christendom.

3. Liturgical. The liturgical type of church is one which defines itself through its worship rather than through the issuance of confessional statements or the requirement of certain kinds of experience from its members. To belong to this tradition you don't have to have had a datable, quantifiable, and measurable conversion, nor do you have to pass an examination in your theological understanding. To belong to a liturgical church, you have to consent to its rites and ceremonies and to practise your faith in the light of what is proclaimed in them. Anglicanism belongs to this type of tradition.

Our church has attempted to embrace both experience and understanding, but has made neither a norm for membership. We have never found it easy to answer the question, "But what must I *believe*?" Nor have Anglicans been good at offering testimonials to their personal encounter with God. This is not because the Anglican church lacks intellectual clarity, nor because God has not met and transformed each of us personally through Jesus Christ. It is because Anglican spirituality is a liturgical spirituality, and because our liturgy is a living, not a fixed, tradition. Theologically this is expressed by the term *lex orandi, lex credendi* — what is prayed is what is believed. In other words, if you wish to know what Anglicans believe, join us in worship and prayer. What we do is what we are.

Nowhere, for example, is there a statement called "The Anglican Doctrine of Marriage." What we believe about marriage as an ideal (and what many people still experience in practice) is contained in the rite of Holy Matrimony. Similarly, if someone wants to know what our church teaches about life after death, they need only attend a celebration of the funeral liturgy. And so on. Though we do have a document called the "Thirty Nine Articles of Religion" it has never functioned in our tradition as a requirement of belief — except for clergy. It is more of an historical manifesto, outlining the position of our church at the time of the Reformation. (It is omitted from the *Book of Alternative Services*.)

These three types of Christian tradition have produced different kinds of spiritual insight and emphasis. The spirituality of the first group of Christians is primarily affective and personal, leading the believer from the despair of sin to the joy of forgiveness and salvation. The spirituality of the second group is primarily corporate and intellectual. The churches of this tradition have produced religious orders and have achieved great clarity in the teaching of faith. But what of the third group? What is distinctive about the spirituality of liturgical Christians? Let us look at Anglican spirituality as it has been expressed in the Prayer Book and now in the *Book of Alternative Services.*

Spiritual Balance

Anglicans have been shaped and formed by the implicit spirituality of the Prayer Book. The hallmark of this is its balance and moderation. The Prayer Book embraces a variety of spiritual approaches to God, but at the same time treats all of them as partial, to be used together in a unifed way rather than separately and exclusively. It achieves a brilliant via media between affective-personal approaches to God on the one hand, and the corporate-intellectual approach on the other.

The Prayer Book, for instance, has united both Evangelicals and Anglo-Catholics within the same church for over four hundred years. This remarkable achievement was made possible only because Anglican liturgy has consciously tied together two historically separate theological worlds, with their different spiritual emphases. Protestantism rediscovered the power of the word of God and the importance of individual response to it in the drama of salvation. Catholicism has maintained the centrality of grace as God's unmerited gift to humanity, and the importance of belonging to the community of grace which is the church. Anglicanism has asserted the centrality of both word and sacrament, as means of grace, and the importance of both individual response and corporate belonging.

This can perhaps be illustrated by pointing to, of all things, church architecture. Protestant architecture, evident particularly in older European churches, expresses a word-centred spirituality by featuring the pulpit as the focal point of church design. In some buildings the pulpit rises ten to fifteen feet above the congregation, often in the middle of the centre aisle, terrifying in its visual dominance. By contrast, the Lord's table (altar) is frequently insignificant, tucked away inconspicuously as a reminder of the anti-Mass theology of some of the radical reformers. This focus on God's word as the bringer of salvation is often accompanied by an emphasis on God's judgement. In many Presbyterian churches in Scotland, for instance, the arrangement of seats for the church elders behind the pulpit resembles nothing more than a high court of law. There is an imposing forensic severity in the sanctuary area, revealing the lasting influence of John Knox upon Presbyterianism with his theology of coming judgement and his vituperative denunciation of sin.

Catholic architecture, on the other hand, tends to feature the altar as the focal point of church design. In many older buildings, especially the great and ancient cathedrals, it is possible to find as many as twenty or thirty altars in special chapels all around the walls of the enclosure. This expresses the sacramental spirituality of the Catholic tradition. Pulpits tend to be less central or visually striking, though there are exceptions to this, particularly in Germany. The baptismal font usually has some prominence, since baptism is the first of the sacraments in Christian life, and may often be found at the door of the church — symbolizing the washing away of sin and spiritual rebirth as the gateway to salvation — or else in a separate building by itself called a baptistry. Modern catholic architecture, however, reflecting the rediscovered integration of baptism and eucharist, places the font in close proximity to the altar. These changes are not dictated by new artistic tastes or fashions, but by a renewed theological emphasis on Christian initiation in the spiritual life of the church.

Now Anglican architecture, as you might expect, attempts a visual balance between all these elements of Christian ritual. Our tradition has featured neither pulpit nor altar (unless the building was "borrowed" from another church), but gives architectural weight and prominence equally to both. This is an attempt to give visual unity to both word and sacrament. In contemporary Anglican buildings it is common to discover altar, pulpit, font, and lectern set almost equidistant from each other, forming a perfect square or diamond. This four-cornered symbolism seems to express the spiritual completeness of reading, hearing, washing, and receiving. It provides for both personal response and corporate nurture in the Christian pilgrimage. In a modest and subtle way, Anglican architecture invites us to celebrate a faith which is both intellectual assent and spiritual reception, both thoughtful response and transforming experience.

The strength of Protestant spirituality lies in its development of the unique relationship between the individual and God. When a person discovers for him or herself the power of God's love and forgiveness, then the gospel comes alive and the renewal of life is made possible. The strength of Catholic spirituality lies in its development of the unique relationship between the church and God. Though individual faith may wax and wane, the church itself has been gifted with all things necessary for human salvation, and the sheer fact of belonging to the body of Christ is often a source of sufficient grace when personal faith is weak.

These two complementary spiritualities are captured in the two principal versions of the Creed. The Apostles' Creed is a statement of faith using the personal pronoun — "*I* believe in God. . . ." This is the creed used at baptisms, when the sponsors or the catechumen must state their personal commitment to Christ. The Nicene Creed, on the other hand, uses the collective pronoun — "*We* believe in One God. . . ." This is the church's corporate statement of faith, used at principal celebrations of the community such as the Sunday eucharist. It allows individuals who cannot yet affirm all the elements of the creed to make the statement with those who can. By using the *we* form, the liturgy allows us to say, "Though I may not yet believe all these things, I belong to a church which believes them." This is particularly appropriate when a normal Sunday gathering will include many unbaptized enquirers, and those still contemplating their Christian commitment.

Both these spiritualities have been incorporated into Anglican liturgy. The authors of the Prayer Book stressed the importance, for example, of a homily at every eucharist. Whereas Protestant liturgy at the time of the Reformation had made the sermon central to worship, and Catholic liturgy had made receiving communion central to worship, Anglican liturgy balanced both and called for both. The sermon is not the main event in Anglican liturgy (a fact of great comfort for preachers). But the liturgy is not complete without it. Similarly, the act of receiving communion by itself is not the sole reason for celebrating the eucharist. Catholic practice has occasionally descended to this (a corruption called sacramentalism), and is still evident in people who arrive just for communion and leave immediately after, or in priests who walk through hospital rooms posting consecrated bread into patients' mouths.

Anglican spirituality is a creative blend, a synthesis of complementary approaches to God and the nurture of faith, encompassed by the liturgy. Liturgy, of course, is not the sum and content of spirituality. Our relationship with God is not confined to worship. But Anglican tradition has regarded public worship as the focal point of individual prayer and devotion, the source of personal nurture in faith from which believers go out into the world in mission and witness. Individual devotion is sustained by membership in the religious community. At the same time, the community itself is sustained in its spiritual life by the example and witness of individual members. Both the individual and the community are thus linked together in a common spiritual task, and the glue which has maintained this through the years has been the Prayer Book.

Prayer Book Spirituality

In addition to public worship, the Prayer Book provides opportunity for private and family devotions in places outside the church building. Anglicans who use the Prayer Book other than on Sundays know that there are prayers for various occasions, from those for the Ministry to the Sick, to the Forms of Prayer to be Used at Sea, to An Order of Service for Young People, to the Forms of Prayer to be Used in Families. Most of these prayers for various occasions were not in the 1662 edition, but were added into the Canadian revision of 1962. This Prayer Book provides a rich resource for people whose faith is sustained by daily and weekly prayer, as well as for those whose prayer life is confined to the Sabbath.

In fact, Anglican spirituality has been nurtured and sustained by the Prayer Book tradition of regular and disciplined prayer. Each day is framed by the four principal offices (meaning *duties*) of Morning Prayer, Mid-Day Prayers, Evening Prayer, and Compline (the final devotion before bedtime). Most clergy, and many lay people, say at least one of these offices daily, either in private or with other family members. It is a cornerstone of our daily pilgrimage through the joys and sorrows of life, a source of courage and hope, which helps us maintain our baptismal covenant with Jesus Christ in the midst of many distractions and temptations. Anglican spirituality encourages us to see the whole of life as encompassed by prayer, so that all our being and doing may be offered to God. This disciplined and regular practice of prayer is not a chore but a freedom. It helps keep the rest of life in perspective, and liberates us from much unnecessary anxiety and activity.

Every copy of the Prayer Book contains a lectionary for Morning and Evening Prayer, and a table of psalms, so that the scriptures may be read sequentially day by day in the context of personal meditation. The scripture readings are intended to form the basis of intercessory prayer (rather than simply a private list of individual needs) and in this way our prayer life is shaped by the word of God rather than the other way round. A spiritual life which is connected to the Christian community and grounded in scripture is not likely to go far wrong, whereas the person whose relationship with God is entirely subjective and unchecked by any discipline or learning ends up with a self-created religion in a denomination of one.

The Prayer Book, therefore, has served almost the same function for us as did the Rule of Life in monastic orders. It is a regimen or rule designed to focus the activities and events of the day under a common and unifying purpose for the whole of life. It grounds personal faith in scripture, and connects the individual with the worshipping community. It is a canon or measure by which our energies and efforts may be assessed and corrected. Properly used, it is a rich spiritual resource for those who take seriously the pilgrimage of faith.

However, the Prayer Book is limited in the options it offers for personal devotion, and repetitive in its daily offices. Although it was an innovative and highly original piece of work in the sixteenth century, the constant repetition of its unvarying words and phrases is unduly constricting for many Anglicans in the twentieth century. The danger this presents to modern people accustomed to more variety and choice in other areas of life is that a kind of boredom can set in which may undermine daily devotion altogether. For this reason, the *Book of Alternative Services* has expanded the range of options and choices for both private and public worship, creating many more provisions for individuals and communities to celebrate and pray according to the changing circumstances of their situation.

The first-time user of the *Book of Alternative Services* will immediately notice the vast and sometimes confusing range of alternative prayers, litanies, and canticles that demand decision and thought. This is perhaps the most common area of difficulty now being experienced, and some confusion and uncertainty will undoubtedly exist for some time, until the richness of the spiritual resources contained in the new rites is fully appreciated. This will only come with usage and a growing familiarity with the contents and location of these various options in the book. The purpose in including all these variations, however, is to continue the way of balanced and comprehensive spirituality which Anglicanism represents. In this respect, the *Book of Alternative Services* stands firmly in the Prayer Book tradition.

In another important respect, however, it does not. Users of the new rites immediately notice another difference from the older book, one which represents a profound departure from Anglican liturgical tradition. It has to do with the feel of the new rites, the ethos of contemporary services. They seem more joyful, more positive, and more optimistic than the Prayer Book services. There is a noticeable lightness and even happiness in the new rites which seems lacking, almost blasphemous, in the old. This feeling has to do with more than just the way the services are conducted by the presider. Even a good presider has difficulty injecting lightness and optimism into a celebration of the Prayer Book eucharist. It is a difference which has to do with the substance of the new rites. The *Book of Alternative Services* marks a theological departure from the Prayer Book in one important way. It is far less penitential and expresses a much stronger emphasis on the resurrection.

Penitence and Passion

The Prayer Book is thoroughly penitential in tone and content. It reflects the penitential nature of much of the prevailing spirituality of the late Middle Ages. Although the authors of the book made some valiant efforts to soften and amend the sorrowing nature of English spiritual practice — particularly through the introduction of prayers of thanksgiving into Morning Prayer — the words of the older rites display an intense preoccupation with the dangers of sin and death. There are three general reasons for this.

1. The Black Death. First, the Black Death had swept through Europe in the fourteenth century creating death and tragedy on an unprecedented scale. An estimated 500,000 people died of the disease (so called because it turned the victims black) in England alone, and this was catastrophic in a nation which had a population of no more than three or four millions. Church reaction, as well as popular superstition, tended to view the epidemic as divine judgement, and there began a series of efforts to cast out the sin which it was thought must have provoked the anger of God. In Spain and France this took the form of a genocidal attack upon Jews, who were believed to be the cause of the divine wrath.

The Black Death was not the only reason for the acute awareness of human fragility among mediaeval men and women. The "shortness and uncertainty of human life" was evidenced in the high rate of mortality in both childbirth and infancy. Childbirth was a life-threatening experience for women, so much so that the church had a special service to mark a woman's survival. It began:

> Forasmuch as it hath pleased Almighty God of his goodness to give you safe deliverance, and hath preserved you in the great danger of Child-birth; you shall, therefore, give hearty thanks unto God. . . .

It was called "The Churching of Women," and it was a service of thanksgiving not for the new-born life but for the escape from death granted by God's grace to the fortunate mother. In an age when medical knowledge was rudimentary and laced with folklore and superstition, death was a constant outcome of what today are experienced as low-risk events. Further, it seemed natural to attribute the arbitrary character of this outcome to the devil, or even to an angry God, and so a great deal of prayer and spiritual devotion was aimed at seeking the protection of God (as well as seeking the intercession of the saints and the Blessed Virgin) against the evil foe, or at appeasing the divine wrath by offering expiatory acts of worship to gain remission of guilt and sin. There is an obvious expiatory character to the liturgies of this era, and the Prayer Book authors could not have imagined designing new forms of worship without it.

2. Passion Mysticism. In the centuries prior to the Reformation, a popular form of devotion centred on contemplating the wounds and the suffering of the crucified Christ. Though it was more prevalent on the continent of Europe than in Britain, it exercised some influence on English spiritual practice, albeit muted by basic English common sense and distaste for extremes. Passion mysticism, as it is called, was a form of prolonged meditation and prayer upon the event of Good Friday. Its purpose was to lead the soul toward mystical absorption in the redemptive agony of our Lord on the cross. In contemplating the wounds, the bloody sweat, the dreadful pain, and so on, of the passion the soul was thought to appropriate for itself the fruits of Christ's redemption and deliverance from sin.

Though it reached its peak well before the sixteenth century, it was still much practised at the time of the Reformation. Ignatius Loyola, a contemporary of Luther and Calvin and founder of the Jesuits (the driving force of the Roman Catholic Counter-Reformation), required his initiates to devote many hours of contemplation to the pain and gore of Jesus' death. He directs: "I will strive while rising and dressing to arouse sentiments of sorrow and grief within myself because of the great sorrow and suffering of Christ our Lord. . . . I will strive not to permit myself any joyful thoughts, even though they are good and holy, as are those of the resurrection and the glory of heaven. I will rather rouse myself to sorrow, suffering, and deep pain, frequently calling to mind the labours, burdens, and sufferings that Christ our Lord bore from the moment of His birth up to the mystery of His Passion, which I am now contemplating" (from *The Spiritual Exercises*).

Another great mystic of the sixteenth century was the Spanish Carmelite Saint John of the Cross. Famous for his poetry and commentaries on the spiritual life, as well as for being the spiritual director of Saint Teresa of Avila, he dwelt at length on the mystery of suffering and pain, publishing such poems as *Dying Because I Do*

Not Die, *The Dark Night*, and *The Living Flame of Love*, all of which are meditations of the soul's redemption through death. Saint John of the Cross was a romantic, regarding pain as an exquisite thing, a means of spiritual purification and redemption, a sign of the soul's salvation. As a personal discipline, he wrapped a length of barbed wire around his torso and wore this under his clothing, so that his body might not forget Christ's suffering for him day or night. It was discovered only after he was taken ill. In places, the skin had grown over the barbs.

Now English spiritual practice has never been strictly ascetical. These examples of obsessive absorption in our Lord's passion are all drawn from continental Catholicism. But nevertheless, Anglicans were not isolated from the influence of such movements and practices, and they made themselves felt in the worship of our church. The adoration of the cross in the liturgy for Good Friday reveals its influence in the rather morbid preoccupation with the nails and the blood, and there are many hymns from the era — now omitted from modern hymn books — which descend into a kind of spiritual sado-masochism in the conviction that vicarious depression is a necessary element in the celebration of Holy Week.

More particularly, the Prayer Book dwells much more on the crucifixion of Christ than on his resurrection. Our Lord's death and passion claim the focus in the eucharistic prayer, far more than his rising and ascending. The Prayer Book tends to linger on Good Friday to the detriment of Easter (the word *resurrection* occurs only twice in the whole of the eucharist — once in the creed, and once in the eucharistic prayer), and this creates a powerfully sombre mood in the rite. Frequent references to the death of Christ (mentioned five times in the eucharistic prayer alone) and to the merits of his passion and blood, all express a theology of the eucharist which centres its meaning in the cross alone.

This fact, though, is not entirely due to the effects of passion mysticism. It has much to do with the influence of England's greatest theologian, Saint Anselm.

3. *Saint Anselm.* Anselm was Archbishop of Canterbury in the eleventh century. He was a philosopher as well as a bishop, and in 1098 published his most important work, *Cur Deus Homo? (Why*

Did God Become Man?). In this book, Anselm outlined the satisfaction theory of the Atonement, a theory about the purpose of the life and death of Christ which profoundly influenced both English and continental theology and found a permanent expression in Anglicanism through its incorporation into the Prayer Book by Thomas Cranmer.

Briefly, Anselm argued that Christ's passion and death were an act of satisfaction for the outraged majesty of God. Building upon Augustine's earlier description of mankind as "a mass of perdition," he posed the question how such sinful and fallen creatures could escape the damnation which God's righteousness required. Anselm felt that justice, even divine justice, has to be satisfied, for God is the source of all cosmic law and does not contradict his own commandments. He suggested that satisfaction was provided by the self-offering of Christ. By taking the sentence of death upon himself, Christ paid the penalty which rightly should have been suffered by the guilty ones, namely ourselves. Because he himself was innocent of sin, God raised him up and restored him to life, thus satisfying the demands of justice and at the same time saving us from our deserved end.

This is the juridical or satisfaction theory of the Atonement. It suggests the image of a courtroom. God is the judge who must pronounce the sentence of death. Mankind is the defendant, inescapably guilty of the charges. But in the courtroom there is One who pleads the case for the prisoners. Christ is our advocate, the friend of the defendants, who mediates between us and our judge in the hope of gaining a lighter punishment. But justice must be done, or the universe is rendered false (feminist theologians regard this as a very masculine theology). And so the advocate becomes our redeemer by suffering the penalty himself, to satisfy the judge and his righteousness.

This is only one of several theories of the Atonement which can be found in scripture (see below), but it is the one which exercised exclusive influence over English theology at the time of the writing of the Prayer Book. Anselm's stature towered over the authors of the Reformation liturgies, as is evidenced in many words and phrases familiar to Anglicans:

> . . .we have an Advocate with the Father, Jesus Christ the righteous, and he is the propitiation for our sins.
> (*BCP* p.78)

> Grant this, O Father, for Jesus Christ's sake, our only Mediator and Advocate. . . .
> (*BCP* p.76)

> A full, perfect, and sufficient sacrifice, oblation and satisfaction for the sins of the whole world. . . .
> (*BCP* p.82)

These frequent references to Christ as advocate, or lawyer for the defence, recall the courtroom imagery of Anselm's theology of judgement. The language of satisfaction and substitutionary death permeates the Prayer Book, especially the eucharist. This has led to an assumption about worship and liturgy which has been unchallenged among Canadian Anglicans until the appearance of the *Book of Alternative Services.* The assumption is that liturgy is a symbolic and ritual entry into the death of Christ, the purpose of which is to receive again the benefits of the Atonement won by our Lord on the cross. Worship in the Prayer Book is therefore primarily an exercise in repentance. The participant is encouraged to seek forgiveness for sins, to meditate upon the evils of sin and death, and to receive again the assurance of pardon and forgiveness through the sacraments of grace.

A significant result of this is that Anglican spirituality has been very preoccupied with personal guilt. Anglicans have been taught to view themselves as unworthy. Many elements of the old rites conspire to maintain this, from the frequency of confession in almost all the rites (far more frequent than in the early rites of the church), to the penitential kneeling postures imposed throughout by the rubrics. Perhaps the best example of the self-abasement the Prayer Book requires as a suitable indication of reverence among worshippers is the Prayer of Humble Access:

> We do not presume to come to this thy Table, O merciful Lord, Trusting in our own righteousness, But in thy manifold and great mercies. We are not worthy so much as to gather up the crumbs under thy Table.
> (*BCP* p.83)

The prayer suggests we are mere grovellers in the courts of heaven, like dogs that eat crumbs from under the master's table (Jesus' description of the Canaanite woman in Matthew 15: 26). This is underscored by the requirement that communion be received kneeling, and that prayer and blessings be undertaken in the same posture.

The effect of this liturgical tradition has been to create in Anglicans a penitential spirituality, a withdrawal into self, a preoccupation with personal guilt and personal salvation. The relative absence in our worship of any balancing emphasis on Easter, on spiritual community, on the gift of new life, on human existence made joyful through the love of Christ, and on the galvanizing power of the Spirit thrusting us outward into the world, has left us spiritually introverted and with a tendency to view ourselves poorly, as miserable sinners unworthy to rejoice in the presence of God.

Furthermore, the relative absence in our worship of a tradition of joyful praise and thanksgiving has tended to make our worship appear to outsiders as somewhat sombre and gloomy (albeit splendid and dignified gloom). The principal exception to this is Morning Prayer which is a liturgy of praise and joy. Anglicans have been nurtured by this rite for many years, especially in parishes where it has been the principal Sunday service, and this may be in no small part due to the fact that it lacks the profoundly penitential character of the Prayer Book eucharist and expresses the more positive feeling of Christian joy in the house of the Lord.

Penitential spirituality, when it lacks a balancing sense of celebration and joyfulness, creates in people an inward disposition to self-doubt and anxiety. Every priest has to undertake the task of counselling such damaged souls, teaching them the art of proper self-love and confidence in the unconditional grace of God. This attitude makes for poor evangelists also, since our retiring and undemonstrative style of faith is ill-suited for proclaiming the good news of Jesus Christ in the marketplaces of the modern world. Further, Anglicans have a penchant for regarding religion as a private and interior matter, unrelated to the world of politics and social change, because they have been shaped by a liturgical tradition which taught that spirituality is about self-abasement, seeking absolution, and securing a place in the afterlife.

These comments are not meant to denigrate the spiritual life of anyone raised on the Prayer Book. I am well aware that for millions of people it has been a rich and sustaining source of spiritual growth. Indeed, I am one of them. My point is that liturgy shapes our spirituality, our relationship with God. The old rites of our church, emerging from the context of the Reformation and containing many of the theological assumptions of the late Middle Ages, has profoundly influenced the way Anglicans think of themselves, their world, and the God who meets them in their daily prayer. For most of us this influence is unconscious. We have never looked critically at the subtle images and assumptions we have been immersed in for these many years.

The *Book of Alternative Services* is changing that. The new rites of our church present a different spiritual emphasis, and express a broader theological position. This is the reason why the new liturgies have a different feel to them. Let's take a look at the implicit spirituality of the *Book of Alternative Services.*

The Recovery of Easter and Pentecost

The church in the apostolic era was filled with a sense of the pervasive presence of the Holy Spirit. In the months and years after Pentecost, the small Jerusalem community grew in confidence, faith, and numbers. The gospel of Jesus began to spread to the surrounding towns and cities, and it eventually travelled throughout the eastern Mediterranean to Rome itself. This monumental task was not achieved by human effort alone. The Book of Acts, which records this development, reveals how the early church felt these events to be the will of the Spirit. The first Christians regarded themselves as instruments of the Spirit's power.

This small company of the faithful faced overwhelming odds. They were despised and attacked by the larger Jewish population (which saw them as heretics), and treated with indifference, and sometimes hostility, by the sophisticated Greek and Roman peoples. But they were still bathed in the radiance of the resurrection. They experienced a strength in this adversity which convinced them of the rightness of their purpose. Though the second and subsequent generations of Christians had not known Jesus in the flesh, nevertheless they knew that their extraordinary survival and growth was due to the presence among them of the risen Christ. They received courage and confidence from him whom God had raised, and who had imparted to them the gift of his Spirit.

It is this sense of the indwelling power of the Spirit and the presence of the risen Christ which the *Book of Alternative Services* attempts to restore to the contemporary church. The new rites are designed for Christians who find themselves once again in an indifferent and sometimes hostile environment. They seek to recapture that confidence and optimism which marked the early church, and which saw it through the trials and difficulties of those critical years. By placing its spiritual focus on the resurrection of Christ and the gifting of the church by the Spirit, the *Book of Alternative Services* has undertaken a deliberate shift of spiritual emphasis. Its purpose is to equip Christians for a time in which they are once again a minority. The theological assumption on which this is based is that resurrection, not crucifixion, must be the central paradigm for a marginalized church in an alienated society.

There are many illustrations of this shift of emphasis in the new liturgies. The dismissal at the close of the eucharist is an exhortation to people to go from the altar of God out into the world rejoicing in the power of the risen Christ and of the Spirit:

May we, who share his body,
live his risen life;
we, who drink his cup,
bring life to others;
we, whom the Spirit lights,
give light to the world.
(*BAS* p.215)

The baptism service balances out the Prayer Book's exclusive emphasis on baptism as participation in the death of Christ by expressing the act as an entry into his death and resurrection:

We give you thanks for sending your Son Jesus. . . . For us he suffered the baptism of his own death and resurrection, setting us free from the bondage of sin and death, and opening to us the joy and freedom of everlasting life.

We give you thanks for your Holy Spirit who teaches us and leads us into all truth, filling us with his gifts so that we might proclaim the gospel to all nations and serve you as a royal priesthood.
(*BAS* p.157)

The rites for Holy Week make this emphasis even clearer. In this most solemn week, our tradition has been to enter deeply into the passion of our Lord and to experience vicariously his humiliation. It has tended to become an occasion for grovelling and self-revilement, with liturgies that are frequently morbid and occasionally depressing. But the *Book of Alternative Services* sets a more uplifting and joyful tone. The new Holy Week services point us beyond the tragedy of the events they commemorate to the glory they ushered in. They express the suffering and humiliation of our Lord as primarily a prelude to his rising and ascending. For example, the celebration on Maundy Thursdays begins:

This is the day
that Christ the Lamb of God
gave himself into the hands of those who would slay him.

This is the day
that Christ gathered with his disciples in the upper room.

This is the day
that Christ took a towel
and washed the disciples' feet,
giving us an example that we should do to others
as he has done to us.

This is the day
that Christ our God gave us this holy feast,
that we who eat this bread
and drink this cup
may here proclaim his Holy Sacrifice
and be partakers of his resurrection,
and at the last day may reign with him in heaven.
(*BAS* p.304)

This introduction recalls the church to its servant ministry, and points us to the glory which Christ has gained by his diaconal faithfulness. Further, it reminds us of the power and strength we receive from the eucharistic community, and expresses a vision of the heavenly kingdom of which the church on earth is to be a symbol and sign.

The Holy Week rites in the *Book of Alternative Services* move us well away from the dark and sorrowing mood of the Prayer Book. Theologically, they are grounded in the fourth gospel. Saint John — far more explicitly than the other evangelists — presents the cross as the fulfilment of Christ's glory, the crowning moment of his life and ministry. His vision of our Lord's death is at the same time a vision of his glorification. The lifting up of Jesus on the cross was the lifting up of mankind in the act of the world's redemption.

It is this unified Johannine vision of life emerging from death that the *Book of Alternative Services* tries to express. In these rites the passion and the victory of our Lord are inseparably intertwined. There is harmony beween his suffering and his triumph. Crucifixion and the exaltation are both dimensions of a single event which have one redemptive meaning. Not even the cruelty of the nails and the wound of the spear are allowed to obscure the essentially expectant mood of the Good Friday liturgy:

We glory in your cross, O Lord,
And praise and glorify your holy resurrection;
for by virtue of your cross
joy has come to the whole world.
(from anthem 2 — p.316)

We adore you, O Christ, and we bless you,
Because by your holy cross you have redeemed the world.

If we have died with him, we shall live with him;
if we endure, we shall also reign with him.
We adore you, O Christ, and we bless you,
because of your holy cross you have redeemed the world.
(from anthem 3 — p.317)

This theme permeates the whole season of Lent, right from its beginning on Ash Wednesday. In fact, nothing illustrates the difference between the old rites and the new so much as the season of Lent itself. The Lenten sevices in the Prayer Book were a preparation for the passion of Christ, whereas the rites in the *Book of Alternative Services* are a preparation for the celebration of Easter. The exhortation which begins the Lenten season makes this clear:

Dear Friends in Christ,
every year at the time of the Christian Passover
we celebrate our redemption
through the death and resurrection
of our Lord Jesus Christ.
Lent is a time to prepare for this celebration
and renew our life in the paschal mystery.
(from the Ash Wednesday liturgy p.281)

Preparing to celebrate the resurrection inevitably sets a different tone to the six weeks of Lent than having a lengthy build-up to the passion. Whereas Holy Week was formerly the climax of Lent, now the goal and object is Easter Day. Where the old rites made penitence the entire purpose of devotion during this time, the new rites see penitence as one aspect of the season, which is to be marked by other forms of devotion too, such as works of charity, self-examination, meditating upon the scriptures, fasting, and prayer:

We begin our journey to Easter with the sign of ashes,
an ancient sign,
speaking of the frailty and uncertainty of human life,
and marking the penitence of the community as a whole.

I invite you therefore, in the name of the Lord,
to observe a holy Lent
by self-examination, penitence, prayer,
fasting, and almsgiving,
and by reading and meditating on the word of God.
(Ash Wednesday liturgy p.282)

Notice that the words of invitation call the people to a corporate observation of the season, not simply to a private and interior preparation. The whole parish or community is invited to journey to Easter, by looking at its life, its mission and ministry, by entering upon a process of renewal and the re-ordering of its goals and priorities. Lent is an excellent time for a parish-life conference, or a well-planned mission. The focus should be not so much on self-denial (I have always thought it strange to give something up for Lent and then start doing it again on Easter Day!), as on preparing to welcome the risen One, and making the new life in Christ visible in the congregation.

Thus the penitential atmosphere of the season is transformed into one of anticipation and excitement. The mood of impending dread gives way to an outlook of mounting celebration. (This was always true of the Prayer Book's treatment of Advent, the other major preparatory season. We have never really found it in ourselves to be gloomy before Christmas. Perhaps this is why Advent has been more popular among Anglicans than Lent. But one wonders why the latter has been less joyful than the former when it is clearly the more important of the two.) The new rites make penitence the point of entry into Easter rather than a vicarious experience of the cross. This is not to denigrate penitence, but to clarify its purpose. Penitence should not be a spiritual end in itself, but only a means to the new life in Christ, which is the true end of all devotion.

Sundays after Pentecost

One of the more confusing aspects of the new book to long-time Anglicans is the disappearance of the season of Trinity. Instead of this, we now have an extended season of Pentecost, which formerly lasted only seven days until Trinity Sunday, but now extends right through the rest of the liturgical year until Advent. This change in the calendar is a sign of the recovery of a focus on the Spirit for the post-Christendom church. There are two reasons for the introduction of Sundays after Pentecost.

First, Pentecost is a much older and more biblically attested event than the Feast of the Holy Trinity. Of course, the mystery of the Godhead is not less significant than the galvanizing power of the Holy Spirit. But it was the latter more than the former which provided the missionary dynamism of the early church. It was the more settled and established times of the Constantinian era, which provided a more leisurely opportunity for the philosophical contemplation of the divine nature, in which the Trinity came to dominate the church's liturgical year. The restoration of Pentecost in the modern calendar is a recognition of our need to recover the dynamism of the Spirit in an age which is no longer settled or established.

Second, it is through the Spirit that we enter another dimension of time. In the liturgy we look backwards to a time that is gone, that is, to the earthly life of Jesus, but which through the Spirit becomes present. And we look forward to the time that is to come, that is, to the final dawning of God's kingdom, but which through the Spirit is brought near. Worship unites these past and future things, and makes us one with both what has gone and what is to come. There are two technical words which express this: *prolepsis* and *anamnesis*. Liturgy is proleptic in that it takes us forward into what has not yet happened. We become guests momentarily at the heavenly banquet. It is an anamnesis (literally, a making present) of what has long gone in that it takes us back to the Last Supper and finds us seats at that historic table with our Lord before his glorification.

One of the purposes of liturgy, therefore, is to provide opportunity for the people of God to be caught up in the Spirit. The revision in the calendar is a way of making this fact more explicit. It asks us to see ourselves as a people gifted by the Paraclete, still guided and sustained by that original Pentecostal fire. Also, it has the consequence of simplifying the liturgical year for better understanding. We can now see that our year of worship begins with Advent and reaches its climax at Easter, and thereafter continues in the presence of the Spirit, the gift of the risen One. Thus the spiritual focus of the *Book of Alternative Services* is grounded in the Easter/Pentecost season, and this is made the focal point of both public and private devotion throughout the year.

Standing Posture

As already noted, the Prayer Book imposed a penitential posture upon Anglicans from the beginning, requiring us to kneel for prayer, communion, and for the receiving of blessings. This was consistent with its theological understanding of our essential unworthiness in the presence of God (even after our redemption by

Christ and our baptism in the Spirit). Curiously, this was a practice opposed by the Calvinist school at the time of the writing of the first and second Prayer Books. They felt that kneeling was an inappropriate posture. Instead, they favoured sitting or standing (though their reasons had less to do with any doubts over penitence than with a deeply rooted suspicion that kneeling was Catholic and idolatrous).

The *Book of Alternative Services*, however, consistent with its different spiritual emphasis, suggests standing as the appropriate posture in the presence of God for those who have been called into Christ's kingdom. Symbolically, this gives physical dramatization to the Easter event. God has raised us from death to life in Christ. We are bidden to stand and rejoice in God's house. Our bodies proclaim what our lips and hearts celebrate, that we have been made worthy through Christ to be called children, heirs, and co-workers with the Lord of creation. Whereas the Prayer Book encouraged self-abasement, the new rites announce:

We offer you this bread and this cup,
giving thanks that you have made us worthy
to stand in your presence and serve you.
(from eucharistic prayer 2 - p.196)

This is not intended to express a false confidence, the narcissism of the Me Generation. It is not saying we are as good as God and so ought not to bow down. (I have a cartoon in my study showing a businessman standing by his bed, hands folded in prayer, saying, "You understand, God, a man in my position doesn't *kneel*.") What this is saying is that *after Easter* our reverence may be expressed in celebration rather than self-abnegation. Because of Christ's faithfulness, not our own, we can have confidence in the presence of God. Easter has changed everything, including our physical attitude.

Architecturally, the consequence of this more optimistic spirituality may eventually be the disappearance of altar rails. As new structures are built to contain the new rites there will be less need for this familiar piece of apparatus, except where there is a desire to retain the option for receiving communion in the traditional manner. Altar rails, in fact, have not always been part of the

Anglican heritage. They were introduced by Archbishop Laud during the English Restoration to protect altars from despoliation by Protestant extremists. They resemble nothing so much as a fence around the sanctuary, separating the people of God from the inner sanctum of the clergy. Such symbolism sits ill with the *Book of Alternative Services.*

Daily Prayer

Regular and disciplined daily prayer, however, remains the cornerstone of Anglican spiritual practice. The *Book of Alternative Services* continues and strengthens the Prayer Book traditon of framing each day with the principal daily offices. But where the old offices were frequently repetitive, the new ones offer a rich and abundant variety of spiritual resources for praise, intercession, and song.

New to Anglicans is the extended number of introductory responses, responsories, canticles, and sentences to be found on pages 72–132. These spiritual treasures are unique to the Canadian church, and have no parallel in other liturgical revisions anywhere in the Anglican communion to date. They are designed to offer a rich daily and seasonal fare for the spiritual gourmet, and are offered for use at Morning and Evening Prayer along with twenty seasonal litanies and forms of intercession. The bewildering plethora of options now available to us in the offices is initially daunting, and may appear as incomprehensible to novices as a Turkish railway timetable. But it simply means that our daily prayer must now be planned and thought out beforehand. Wise and careful use of the resources for prayer in the *Book of Alternative Services* will ensure a flexible and sound spiritual diet, unlikely to descend into boredom.

There is, of course, a separate lectionary for the daily office (on pages 452–497) which — unlike the Prayer Book, which lists them in another place — contains the psalms for the day along with the readings. In addition, the new book provides a lectionary for the weekday eucharist which is different from that of the daily office. This is for those worthy and stalwart souls who say morning and evening prayer at home and attend midweek celebrations of the eucharist with their local community as well. One might have wished that these lectionary lists had appeared at the back of the book instead of the middle. They tend to be where the book falls open, presenting the casual browser with a startling array of indecipherable hieroglyphics, unwelcoming of further curiosity.

Also a little confusing is the fact that Compline, one of the favourite offices of spiritual veterans, appears to have disappeared altogether. In fact, it hasn't. It is buried in the options for Evening Prayer under the headings for late evening (see the second paragraph of the rubrics on page 60). The reason for this appears to be that the new book attempts to return to an earlier practice in the church of having two daily offices rather than four. Personally, I regret this. It adds an unnecessary complication to the already difficult task of sorting out the page numbers and locations of things, and disperses a popular Anglican service throughout a general and scattered series of variations.

However, there are rich and extended forms of prayer for use on different occasions in families and in the home (see pages 687-697). These include forms of group prayer which may incorporate the sharing of a meal, or which centre around the Advent wreath, or on the anniversary of a baptism, or on the occasion of a family member leaving home. On page 694 there are twelve forms of grace at meals, which should come in handy for those individuals rendered speechless by sudden and unexpected invitations to say the blessing before dinner. In general, the *Book of Alternative Services* contributes most helpfully to the nurture of Christian family worship, and will be of great assistance to those parents who take seriously the task of Christian education in the home.

Atonement in the *Book of Alternative Services*

It is apparent now that the new rites are less dependent on the theological models of the late Middle Ages, and reach back to the liturgical resources of a much earlier time when the outlook of Christians was less penitential and more joyful. This has led some conservative critics to pronounce the contemporary rites "weak on sin" or guilty of "diluting the Atonement." But nothing could be further from the truth.

In the New Testament we cannot find any single and systematic statement of the work of Christ. The doctrine of the Atonement, which is an attempt to define what our Lord achieved and accomplished for us, is a product of later Christian reflection. What we do find in the New Testament is a series of images and word pictures which offer different ways to understand both who Jesus is, and what he has done for mankind. These images run in and around each other in fluid patterns. It is possible to discern four basic models of the work of Christ in the New Testament, but while we may separate them out for purposes of distinguishing them, they are not so separated in the New Testament. These four biblical models all intermingle in scripture, and together make up what we call today the Atonement. It is worth surveying them briefly because each of them appears in the *Book of Alternative Services*.

1. Christ as Obedient Servant. The theme of our Lord's obedience unto death is expressed in many passages in the New Testament. For example:

> Because of this humble submission his prayer was heard: son though he was, he learned obedience in the school of suffering, and, once perfected, became the source of eternal salvation for all who obey him. (Hebrews 5: 7-9)

This image is one of a cluster of images whch portray our Lord as the suffering servant (a figure which first appears in the Old Testament in the Book of Isaiah), whose righteousness in the face of temptations has rendered righteous those who submit themselves to his gracious leading. The image suggests that through his obedience we are made acceptable before God. Similar suggestions occur in Hebrews 2: 10 and Romans 5: 19.

In the *Book of Alternative Services* this theme is expressed in several places, for instance, in the words of eucharistic prayer 2:

> In fulfilment of your will
> he stretched out his hands in suffering,
> to bring release to those who place their hope in you;
> and so he won for you a holy people.
>
> He chose to bear our griefs and sorrows,
> and to give up his life on the cross,
> that he might shatter the chains of evil and death,

and banish the darkness of sin and despair.
By his resurrection
he brings us into the light of your presence.
(*BAS* p.196)

This prayer captures both the image and the specific wording of the suffering servant text in Isaiah 53. It suggests that our reconciliation with God is made possible through his obedience and constancy unto death. By belonging to Christ through faith, aided by grace, we participate in the victory over evil and death which he won for us by giving up his life.

2. Christ as Sacrifice. The theme of the shedding of his blood as a sacrifice for the sin of the world is another of the scriptural images of Christ's work. For example:

The blood of his sacrifice is his own blood, not the blood of goats and calves; and thus he has entered the sanctuary once and for all and secured an eternal deliverance . . . he offered himself without blemish to God, a spiritual and eternal sacrifice; and his blood will cleanse our conscience from the deadness of our former ways and fit us for the service of the living God. (Hebrews 9: 12–14)

This theme has important roots in Jewish ritual and spirituality. It refers to the practice of offering up an (animal) sacrifice as expiation for human sin and guilt. The death of an innocent, it was thought, restored innocence to the people. Temple sacrifices were a significant aspect of worship in Jesus' time, and after the resurrection his Jewish followers in particular came to understand his life and death as an act of cosmic sacrifice. His blood, shed by the guilty, purified the world of its guilt. On finds the analogy also in Ephesians 5: 2.

In the *Book of Alternative Services* this sacrificial image is less prominent than in the Prayer Book ("and our souls washed through his most precious blood"), but it does appear in such places as eucharistic prayer 1:

Gracious God,
his perfect sacrifice

destroys the power of sin and death;
by raising him to life
you give us life for evermore. . . .

Send your Holy Spirit upon us
and upon these gifts,
that all who eat and drink at this table
may be one body and one holy people,
a living sacrifice in Jesus Christ our Lord.
(*BAS* p.194 –195)

Also, in eucharistic prayer 3:

We pray you, gracious God,
to send your Holy Spirit upon these gifts,
that they may be the sacrament
of the body of Christ
and his blood of the new covenant.
Unite us to your Son in his sacrifice,
that we, made acceptable in him,
may be sanctified by the Holy Spirit.
(*BAS* p.199)

One of the points of great contention during the Reformation
was the idea of the "sacrifice of the Mass." Many Catholic scholars
at the time held that every time the Mass was celebrated Christ was
sacrificed again. Anglicanism, under Anselm's earlier influence, rejected this theology as unscriptural and abhorrent. Christ, according to the epistle to the Hebrews, had been sacrificed once for all,
and so Anglican theology has held the eucharist to be a memorial
(*anamnesis*) of that sacrifice. The Prayer Book makes this point
strongly in the consecration prayer (quoted above), and the *Book
of Alternative Services* stands firmly in line with it. These prayers
indicate that Christ's sacrifice is indeed sufficient and never to be
repeated, and ask that we who participate in this sacrament may be
united with him in that sacrifice, so that our lives may be offered up
in thanksgiving with his.

3. Christ as Satisfaction. This theme is the principal model of the
work of Christ portrayed in the Prayer Book. It is the same as

Anselm's Juridical Theory (see above), and a few Anglicans seem to think it is the only proper model of the Atonement. However, though it is certainly one of the biblical images, it is not the only one. Its scriptural base is found in Paul's letter to the Romans, for example:

It is God's way of righting wrong, effective through faith in Christ for all who have such faith — all, without distinction. For all alike have sinned, and are deprived of the divine splendour, and all are justified through God's free grace alone, through his act of liberation through the person of Christ Jesus. For God designed him to be the means of expiating sin through his sacrificial death, effective through faith. God meant by this to demonstrate his justice. . . .(Romans 3: 21–25)

Enough has been said of this model above. The Prayer Book is permeated with the language of satisfaction and substitution, and though this is not absent from the *Book of Alternative Services*, it does not have its former prominence, and is largely absent from the eucharistic prayers.

4. Christus Victor. This is the theme found most richly in the fourth gospel, the victory of Christ over the cosmic powers of evil and death through the triumph of the cross:

'Now is the hour of judgement for this world; now shall the Prince of this world be driven out. And I shall draw all men to myself, when I am lifted up from the earth.' This he said to indicate the kind of death he was to die. (John 12: 31–33)

The theme is repeated in the letter to the Colossians:

On that cross he discarded the cosmic powers and authorities like a garment; he made a public spectacle of them and led them as captives in his triumphal procession. (Colossians 2: 15)

This image presents the death and resurrection of Jesus as the end of the cosmic struggle between darkness and light. By raising Christ to life, God has broken the power of Satan over human mortality. Death is ended, and mankind can go free. Christ the King is crowned in triumph and raised up in glory, and the cross, from being an instrument of tragedy, is now presented to the world as something sublime in its beauty. Other examples of the theme in the New Testament are to be found in Ephesians 6: 12 and Hebrews 2: 14.

We have already discussed how the glorification of our Lord is extensively presented in the *Book of Alternative Services*. Of all the biblical models of the work of Christ, this seems to be the principal choice of its authors. The transformation of despair into courage, of alienation into hope, and of weakness into joy is the spiritual purpose of this emphasis. It is expressed in eucharistic prayer 1 thus:

> Dying you destroyed our death,
> rising you restored our life.
> Lord Jesus, come in glory.
> (*BAS* p.195)

And in eucharistic prayer 6:

> To fulfil your purpose
> he gave himself up to death
> and, rising from the grave, destroyed death
> and made the whole creation new.
>
> And that we might live no longer for ourselves,
> but for him who died and rose for us,
> he sent the Holy Spirit,
> his own first gift to those who believe,
> to complete his work in the world,
> and to bring to fulfilment
> the sanctification of all.
>
> When the hour had come for him to be glorified
> by you, his heavenly Father,
> having loved his own who were in the world,
> he loved them to the end. . . .
> (*BAS* p.208)

None of these images of Atonement is complete in itself, but all of them together impress upon the prayerful heart the enormous grace of our Lord's dying and rising. In presenting all of them in their diversity and richness, along with many images of the ministry of Jesus among the poor and broken-hearted, the *Book of Alternative Services* creates a diverse and fertile soil for spiritual growth. The comprehensiveness of these scriptural models, and the broader theological basis they provide, precludes fixation on any particular doctrine of the work of Christ and allows a wider spiritual exploration of our biblical heritage. This in turn opens the possibility of new approaches to prayer.

The spirituality of the *Book of Alternative Services* thus continues the best of the Anglican tradition established in the Prayer Book, but broadens and balances it in a conscious effort to equip the people of God for the challenge of a new world. It espouses no particular theory or school of spiritual journeying. It shows no commitment to passing theologies or to individual positions. In fact, there is something quite ancient about this modern book.

Instead, it tries to maintain characteristic Anglican tolerance and moderation. It seeks to encompass the diversity and plurality of contemporary Christianity, without vagueness or ambivalence. For this reason it will not satisfy flag-wavers for particular causes or single-minded occupants of isolated hilltops. It is, after all, a set of rites for the church as a whole. It could not do less than respect the diversity that already exists among us.

The implicit spirituality in the book is a more confident and optimistic one than we have inherited from the declining years of Christendom. Perhaps this may seem inappropriate. Why should we be confident when we have become such a marginal reality in contemporary society? We do so because we have been given a pearl of great price. We are the ambassadors of the gospel of life. The Lord of the universe has imparted to us a message of salvation and peace, and the gates of hell shall not prevail against it. This alone gives us hope. The risen Christ still meets us in worship and prayer. With this truth to assure us, we can take some comfort in our marginality, and perhaps as a church we may begin to regain our nerve.

Questions for Discussion

1. What influences have shaped your spiritual life? What do you find most nurturing of your relationship with God?

2. Do you think that Anglican preaching and worship has concentrated on sin and guilt to the detriment of praise and joy?

3. What sort of worship do you most enjoy?

4. Create a service of prayer (right now!) among your group using the resources in the *Book of Alternative Services* for the daily office. Plan it together. Look at the options among the canticles, responsories, and litanies on pages 72 to 132. Find the lections and the psalms for the day. Appoint readers, cantors, intercessors, and a leader. Go on. Explore and enjoy!

6. Ministry

God of faithfulness,
in every age you call men and women
to make known your love.
May we who celebrate this eucharist today
be so strengthened in the ministries to which we are called,
that we may always witness to your holy name.
(from the propers for Ember Days: *BAS* p.396)

The Ministry of the Whole People of God

Ministry is a word traditionally applied to the ordained only.
When Anglicans have thought about ministry they have usually
imagined it to be something done by the clergy, an activity of the
ordained toward the non-ordained. Until recently, if lay people
thought of themselves in connection with ministry at all, it was
normally in terms of their relationship with the clergy. For many
years, lay people have considered themselves to be merely the
recipients of ministry — even, sometimes, excluded from it.

In the contemporary church, however, there has been a growing
awareness among both ordained and non-ordained alike that
ministry is the work of the whole people of God. We are recovering
a truth that the early church knew well, that all of us are called to
be ministers of the gospel and ambassadors of Christ in the world.
It was upon this knowledge that the pre-Christendom church built
up its life in community, and took the good news of Jesus Christ
out into the world with such success. The first Christians
understood themselves to be a people gifted in diverse ways by the
Spirit and called to a variety of ministries, both lay and ordained,
each one contributing to the life of the body. The emergence again
in the post-Christendom church of this understanding of the variety
of ministries among both clergy and laity is the result of several
factors arising from the modern situation.

First, we see the beginnings of a long-overdue recognition of the gifts of the laity. The church is becoming aware that in every congregation there is a vast range of talents and abilities which God has provided in that community. These are not vested in a few individuals alone, but are spread throughout the people, who are gathered in that place as a kind of talent bank ready to be used by our Lord for ministry. Skilled leadership of such communities aims at identifying, organizing, and releasing that energy for the work of mission and evangelism. Where this leadership exists, laity are encouraged to discover their gifts and to see themselves as engaged in ministry wherever their daily work or responsbility might be. Where it does not exist, people may not come to see themselves as ministers of Christ in the world at all, and the vast reservoir of human resources in the parish is squandered in under-employment.

The equipping of the people of God for ministry is still a slow development, however. Christian tradition is ill-suited for it. During the Christendom years of the church, ministry became professionalized. The clergy were shaped into an educated class for a largely uneducated and illiterate laity. They took over the work of ministry by virtue of their training and knowledge. Though there were periodic attempts to reverse this ghettoization of ministry in the form of large and popular lay movements (mostly monastic movements, such as that of Saint Francis of Assisi), they enjoyed only marginal success. The lay monastic movements were quickly absorbed into the professional structure of the church. Religious orders became a professional form of ministry in themselves.

In the post-Christendom context, however, clergy no longer form an educated elite. They are members of a society which provides high levels of education and specialized training to large numbers of people. In many congregations, ordained clergy are academically less qualified than many laity, and must learn the skill of utilizing the abilities of lay people without feeling dwarfed by their talents. (In my present parish, for example, there is a dazzling array of education among the members. So much so, that I hesitate to wear an academic hood on Sundays, lest the congregation should decide to turn up in theirs as well!)

Second, there is a growing recognition of the historic importance of lay ministry in the development of the church in Canada. As we prepare to celebrate the two-hundredth anniversary of the arrival in Nova Scotia of Charles Inglis, the first Anglican bishop in

Canada, it is worth remembering that the church in this country was not built by clergy, but by clergy and laity together. In the early years of European settlement, lay people often did the pioneering work which prepared the ground for the later arrival of professional clergy. Wives of settlers taught Bible schools, men conducted services, lay missionaries trekked through the forests and canoed the rivers from Newfoundland to Kingston long before Inglis arrived.

The history of Anglicanism in Canada is the story of efforts by both lay and ordained people (with the aid of overseas missionary societies) working together to bring our particular style of theology and worship to this vast land. It was the indispensable contribution of lay people to this work that led to the formation of synodical government here decades before its emergence in the Church of England. The first General Synod in Canada met in Trinity College, Toronto in 1893, while in England the same system of (lay and clergy) government was introduced only in 1970. The participation of lay people in the decision-making councils of the church has been a unique feature of Canadian Anglicanism, a fact which, in the end, was bound to undermine the clericalization of ministry.

A third factor in the recovery of shared ministry has been the growth of non-stipendiary ministries. In several places, with the support of the diocesan bishop, remote communities which cannot support paid professional clergy are turning to ordained but unpaid persons as an alternative way of providing spiritual and pastoral leadership. Though the impetus for non-stipendiary ministry is economic, its basis is soundly biblical. Saint Paul was not paid for his missionary efforts, but while he travelled made his living as a tent-maker. The first Christian communities were led by women and men whom the community recognized as having particular spiritual gifts, and who were set apart through sacred rites for the exercise of ministry in the communities in which they already lived, without any particular remuneration.

The emergence of non-stipendiary ministries in today's highly specialized and professionally-minded society is forcing the church to take a critical look at its whole system of selection and training of clergy. The ancient practice in the Christian community of identifying spiritual leaders from among its own members is quite different from the model of leadership development we have inherited from Christendom. It presents quite a separate theology of ministry and of authority, and is gaining some attention from church leaders. Let me explain.

Since the development of ordained ministers as a separate professional class, the church's practice has been to wait for individuals to identify themselves as having a vocation to orders. Then they are taken out of their local community, sent away for professional training, and later parachuted into a totally different community with a stipend and a certificate of authority. This model has tended to promote the distancing of ordained and non-ordained members of the body from another, with the consequent diminishing of the ministry of the laity.

Interestingly, the more ancient practice of the church, whereby the community identified its leaders and set them apart by sacred rites, is similar to the pattern of selection of spiritual leaders in the native cultures of Canada. Shamans or holy men were those obviously gifted with power from the Great Spirit. Their authority came not from any external authentication, but from the natural or inner authority they possessed, which was confirmed and accepted by the people. The recent revival of traditional native spirituality in Canada has brought this model of appointment and authorization to the attention of church leaders, particularly those in areas where Christianity and native culture are in close relationship. It is perhaps not surprising that some of the more creative thinking about ministry in Canada is being done by the Council of the North, those dioceses which face economic difficulties and at the same time are in contact with strong models of community and authority of the pre-Christendom type.

The fourth, and perhaps most important, factor is the renewed emphasis on baptism as the primary sacrament of Christian vocation. Much has already been said about this, and we have seen how the *Book of Alternative Services* restores baptism to a central place in the life of the Christian community (see chapter three). This development results directly from the ecumenical efforts of the churches to find a common ground for Christian unity, and to develop common approaches to ministry. It has led the churches to question the exclusion of baptized lay persons from the practice of ministry, and to affirm the call to ministry of the whole people of God.

Ecumenical discussions aimed at the mutual recognition of sacraments and orders have been forced back again and again to baptism as the starting point of Christian life. It is in baptism that individuals affirm their response to the call of Christ. Here they are made members one of another and undertake the commitment of mutual ministry. In baptism they are gifted by the Spirit for the work of ministry. In this theological perspective, therefore, baptism is the basis of all Christian ministry, both lay and ordained. Every Christian is called to be a minister of the gospel.

The Ordering of Ministries

The ministry of the whole people of God does not, of course, preclude the exercise of specific ministries by persons called to particular roles and functions within the church. Indeed, from the very beginning, the various gifts given by the Spirit to individuals have been differentiated and ordered according to the needs of the church as a whole. Thus, as we read in the New Testament, some were called to be pastors, some teachers, some prophets, some evangelists, some doctors, and so on, in accordance with their various aptitudes. It seems that two kinds of ministry characterized the very first years of the church: the peripatetic ministry of people like Paul (and other evangelists and prophets) who travelled about visiting the different communities scattered around the eastern Mediterranean; and the settled, stationary ministry of pastors, elders, and teachers who remained in their local communities and maintained oversight of the people.

The New Testament word for oversight is *episkope*. The office of bishop as we know it today has evolved from the *episkope* that was exercised over the church by those first called to pastoral responsibility. The first *episkopoi* were overseers, watching over the life of the community committed to their care, maintaining its discipline, and leading its worship. As the church grew outwards, these ministers were given charge over several communities at once, and gradually took over the peripatetic work of the itinerant ministers. In their place, the church appointed *presbyteroi* or elders whose responsibility was to exercise oversight in the absence of the bishop. It is from the word *presbyter* that we derive the term *priest*.

Even before the emergence of the office of presbyter, however, the early church had created the separate order of deacons. Their tasks were to serve the community's needs, particularly the needs of the widows and orphans, and also the sick and the destitute.

Originally, the deacons were appointed as assistants to the bishop and were a distinct order of ministry responsible solely to him. It was only later, as the bishop became less able to exercise direct supervision over them, that the deacons were placed under the authority of the priests.

Thus the threefold orders of bishop, priest, and deacon emerged within the church early on. They were specific ways in which the church ordered its ministry and differentiated between the various gifts for ministry among its members. During the years of Christendom these offices underwent growth and change, with bishops assuming more and more of the work of government in the church, but they maintained their original biblical and apostolic character. After the Reformation in England, the church retained these orders with a few changes. In our tradition, bishops, priests, and deacons continue to exercise responsibility for oversight, care, and service of the members of the body of Christ so that the community may be built up in love.

Ministry and Liturgy

The difficulty has been, however, that the specialized ministries have tended to obscure or even to take over completely from other forms of ministry. This was perhaps inevitable after the beginning of the Constantinian period when the church was able to create within itself the infrastructure of a public institution, and began to order its ministry in a more stratified way. As Christendom developed, the ordained ministries became the object of much attention and study. Episcopal and priestly orders became more distinct from each other (they were not so distinct in apostolic times), and each acquired separate liturgical functions, as did the deacons.

Theologically, the ministry of bishops was linked with that of the apostles, and their authority became grounded in the doctrine of apostolic succession, the unbroken chain of ordination by the laying on of hands that stretched from each bishop back to the disciples of our Lord. The ministry of priests was grounded theologically in the Old Testament. It was derived from the Jewish practice of setting apart a certain order within the community to offer ritual sacrifice to God on behalf of the people. Deacons gained the liturgical role of assisting the priests in this offering, though retaining their primary ministry of service to the community. During these years the church as a whole was evolving a new understanding of itself and its ministry in the context of the empire, and both the responsibility and the authority for this ministry shifted away from the people as a whole to the clergy themselves.

This shift introduced profound changes into the liturgy of the church. A glance at church architecture, for instance, eloquently reveals different phases of lay-clergy relationships. The first type of public building created for Christian worship was the basilica. This consisted of a single room with the altar at one end (sometimes covered by a domed roof) around which the clergy and laity gathered in a semi-circular arrangement. The presence of the whole community together around the altar was a continuation of the pre-Constantinian forms of worship, which were mostly of the house-church type, the community gathering in a single room around a central table. Worship in the basilica involved the laity as well as the clergy.

In the eighth and ninth centuries, however, there emerged an architectural creation called the porch-church. This was still a basilica style, but with the addition of aisles and galleries and external towers. It allowed for many processions and new forms of liturgical movement, such as the adoration of the Blessed Sacrament. But the elaboration of ritual which the porch-church made possible also made worship an increasingly clerical affair. The people became passive onlookers. Professor J.G. Davies explains:

> The passivity of the congregation, which played so important a part in the decline of the porch-church, had, as its obverse, the increasing importance of the clergy, who now ceased to conduct the liturgy 'on behalf of' and celebrated it 'instead of' the congregation. The architectural result of this was that the place of the clergy, which had usually occupied the east end of the nave together with the apse, was removed out of the body of the church to create a second room. Hence the two-room plan of the Middle Ages - the sanctuary being for the ordained ministers, the nave for the laity. In terms of the eucharist, this had involved a shift of emphasis from the communion to the consecration with the elevation as its climax - all that was needed therefore, since non-communicating attendance was widespread, was a distant view of the raised host, dimly glimpsed through the chancel

screen beneath the rood at the far end of the choir. The priest had also moved from facing the people across the altar to standing with his back to them and so looking towards the east (from "Architectural Setting," *A Dictionary of Liturgy and Worship,* J.G. Davies, ed.).

Here we can see the complex interrelation of theology, liturgy, and ministry. The elaboration of ritual after Constantine, together with an emphasis on an Old Testament theology of priesthood, gradually forced the separation of clergy and laity in the action of the liturgy. And not only were the people excluded from participation in the leading of the rites, they eventually ceased to participate in communion itself. By the time of the Reformation, the laity were almost completely non-communicating (which goes a long way to explain the predominance of Mattins in Anglican worship), and this fact became structurally institutionalized in the development of screens separating nave from sanctuary. Again, this was an Old Testament practice (the curtain of the temple, mentioned in the gospels. This curtain was torn in two at the moment of Jesus' death — but the theological and liturgical significance of this was obviously lost in the Christendom era), and its practical effect was to shape the laity into passive recipients of ministry rather than galvanizing them into the exercise of it.

Modern church architecture, however, reflects a post-Constantinian shift back to the participation of the people in worship. Contemporary church buildings are beginning to recover the basilica style, but with the altar moved closer toward the nave, so that clergy and laity are together again in the celebration of the eucharist. In several recent designs, the altar is so placed that clergy and laity completely surround it in a circular pattern, (as, for instance, in the new Roman Catholic cathedral in Liverpool, England) indicating the unbroken unity of the reconciled community in the presence of God. This is symbolic of a shift not only in liturgy, but also in our understanding of ministry. All our ministries, ordained and lay alike, begin and end in community with each other and in the company of Christ. The ordering of ministries arises out of our common calling in baptism and our common nurture in the eucharist.

How then does the *Book of Alternative Services* express this vision of separate ministries, ordered according to the gifts of the Spirit, but shared between ordained and non-ordained? Let us take a look at the rites for the ordering of ministry in the church.

The Ministry of the Laity

Since baptism is the ritual starting-point of Christian discipleship (though not necessarily the chronological one), it provides the basis in worship for the ministry of the *laos*, the whole people of God. In the Prayer Book tradition, baptism is presented as the beginning of the redeemed life, a washing away of sin leading to the inheritance of the fruits of Christ's death. This is a necessary beginning to Christian ministry, but the Prayer Book did little to develop the implications of this sacramental cleansing for the subsequent life and work of the believer. It remains a sacrament primarily signifying divine salvation, the rescuing by God of the lost soul. True, the one so saved is urged to be a soldier for the Lord, and to fight against sin, the flesh, and the devil. But this urging is directed at the interior life of the baptized person, and does not spell out very clearly the responsibility of Christians beyond themselves.

The 1962 revisions to the Canadian Prayer Book made some attempt to incorporate into liturgy the idea of lay ministry, but not in the baptismal rite itself. Instead, it appears in the Supplementary Instruction which was added to the old 1662 Catechism. Candidates for confirmation were to be instructed in the work to which they were called in the church thus:

Question: What is your work as a lay member in the Church of God?

Answer: To take my part in its worship, labours, and councils, according to the gifts of grace that God has given me, and to pray, work, and give for the spread of his kingdom.
(*BCP* p. 554)

The place where the Prayer Book comes closest to outlining a list of responsibilities in lay ministry is in the service of Institution and

Induction of an Incumbent. At the end of this ceremony the bishop says to the people of the parish:

> It is the duty of the people to afford to their Minister at all times all needful help and encouragement in his work, and to give of their substance to his support; so that, being free from wordly anxieties, he may devote himself wholly to the preaching of God's Word and the ministration of the Sacraments. Therefore, I charge and exhort you, Brethren and Churchwardens of this Parish, to pray continually for this your Minister who is set over you in the Lord, and to help him forward in all the duties of his holy calling. Bear ye one another's burdens, and so fulfil the law of Christ.
> (*BCP* p. 676)

This noble exhortation, which one fondly wishes could be repeated regularly at the annual vestry meeting, is nevertheless a poor statement of the fullness of lay ministry. It defines the work of the laity solely in relation to that of the clergy. It confines the ministry of the non-ordained to the spiritual and financial support of the ordained — the minister — so that he can do ministry. We see here at work the Christendom assumptions about the professionalization of ministry which have been part of our liturgical tradition.

By contrast, the *Book of Alternative Services* encourages a much fuller understanding of the variety of ministries within the body of Christ. The rubric which introduces the propers for Ember Days (i.e., prayers which in the old rites were to be said only for those about to be ordained) explains that they are now "to be used at times of prayer for the whole ministry of the Church" (*BAS* p. 395). The collect for Ember Days (from an old English word meaning 'period' — a length of time before major ordination festivals) now reads:

> Almighty God,
> by your grace alone
> we are accepted and called to your service.
> Strengthen us by your Holy Spirit
> and make us worthy of our calling.

The calling to which this points is not simply the vocation to ordained ministry (which, for those about to enter orders, it certainly includes) but also the call to diaconal ministry made to all Christians in baptism. The inclusiveness of this idea is made clear in the prayer after communion. When all have received from the eucharistic table, the celebrant says:

God of our salvation,
your Spirit has given us new life,
and you have nourished us with holy things.
May we be living members of your Son Jesus Christ,
and exercise the ministry to which we are called.
(*BAS* p. 396)

The intention here is not to abandon the practice of prayer for those about to be ordained. Ember Days continue to be a feature of the church's devotion (see the calendar on p. 18). Rather, the intention is to expand the practice to include those who will receive that ministry as well as those who will offer it. It is a way of reminding the church that all Christian life should be expressed in mutual service and prayer, and that all are equipped by the Spirit with gifts for ministry. It incorporates a position taken in the report of the church's Committee on Ministry to General Synod in 1983: "Ordination must be defined in the context and perspective of the total ministry of the whole Laos."

The new baptismal rite is the place where we see the basic elements of lay ministry articulated. This is considerably different from the old initiation rite in the Prayer Book in that it expresses baptism not only as a ritual of purification and cleansing, but also as a commissioning of the person for servanthood. It maintains the Prayer Book emphasis on the renunciation of evil and on turning to Christ as Saviour and Lord, which are the prerequisite commitments of baptism, but extends these to include the commitment to a life of work and witness in the world. The prayers for the candidate(s) make clear the hope the church places in those who come to Christ:

Deliver them, O Lord, from the way of sin and death.
Lord, hear our prayer.

Open their hearts to your grace and truth.
Lord, hear our prayer.

Fill them with your holy and life-giving Spirit.
Lord, hear our prayer.

Teach them to love others in the power of the Spirit.
Lord, hear our prayer.

Send them into the world in witness to your love.
Lord, hear our prayer.

Bring them to the fullness of your peace and glory.
Lord, hear our prayer.
(*BAS* p. 155)

The meaning is apparent here that Christian life involves more than an interior righteousness and faith, but also that this should issue in action and deeds. Again, the promises required from the candidates or their sponsors in the baptismal covenant go much further than the former covenant in the Prayer Book:

Celebrant Will you proclaim by word and example the good
         news of God in Christ?
People   I will, with God's help.

Celebrant Will you seek and serve Christ in all persons, loving
         your neighbour as yourself?
People   I will, with God's help.

Celebrant Will you strive for justice and peace among all people,
         and respect the dignity of every human being?
People   I will, with God's help
         (*BAS* p, 159)

We begin to see that the ministry of the baptized is a ministry of proclamation and justice-making. We are called to make the good news of Christ known in our several places of responsibility, according to our gifts. We are to build the kingdom of God on earth with our lives and labours, wherever we happen to be.

Baptism, therefore, implies the taking up of a specific and intentional ministry wherever we chance to live or work. It invites us to see our workplace — whether that is the home, our school, the office, etc., — as a place where Christ needs to be made known in our actions and words. The new rite encourages us to re-cognize ourselves, that is, to know ourselves again in a different way from before, as ambassadors and ministers of the gospel. Just as Christ was sent into the world by the Father, so we are sent by Christ to continue that ministry of redemption. This is not a ministry that ordained people can take over from the laity. This is specifically a calling to those who live and work outside the institution of the church.

For this reason, it might be useful if Anglicans dropped the term *minister* when referring to the clergy. This word — which in the Prayer Book itself is intended to refer to both lay and ordained persons — obscures the reality of both ordained and lay ministries when it is used in connection with the clergy alone. In our tradition, ordained persons are either bishops, priests, or deacons, and should be referred to as such. I remember when this fact was first impressed upon my mind. I once attended a church in Ottawa, and each Sunday at the front of the leaflet were the words: "This church has 500 ministers, and one priest who is the Reverend. . . ." That was good parish education!

The baptism ceremony in the *Book of Alternative Services* concludes with two important new statements. First, after the water rite there comes the giving of the light. A candle lit from the Paschal candle, which was carried into the church on Easter eve, is presented to each new initiate. The purpose of this symbol is twofold. Primarily, it links the act with Easter. The flame represents the new life of Christ into which the initiate has entered, through participation in his resurrection. Secondarily, it represents the call to ministry. The statement of the people at the giving of the light makes this clear:

Let your light so shine before others
that they may see your good works
and glorify your Father in heaven.
(*BAS* p. 160)

Then, immediately after this statement, there comes another addition to the rite. The initiate is welcomed into the household of God and invited to share in the eternal priesthood of the baptized. This phrase is familiar to members of the Protestant churches, but not quite so familiar to Anglicans. It refers to the idea of the priesthood of all believers, a concept championed by John Calvin in his sixteenth-century polemics against Rome, and to the royal priesthood mentioned in the New Testament (see 1 Peter 2: 9). These phrases apply not to the ordained priests, but to baptized members of the body who share in the great high priesthood of Christ himself. The rite concludes:

> Celebrant Let us welcome the newly baptized.
> People   We receive you into the household of God.
>   Confess the faith of Christ crucified,
>   proclaim his resurrection,
>   and share with us in his eternal priesthood.
>   (*BAS* p. 161)

The priesthood to which this welcomes the initiate is not that of clerical orders. It is an invitation to a life of self-offering and sacrifice, as Christ offered himself in love and service for the world. The New Testament uses the word *priest* (Greek, *hiereus*) only in reference to our Lord himself, who as the great high priest, gave himself as an oblation for the life of the world, and to the community he called into service, who share in his self-giving through baptism. It is of the essence of priesthood to offer sacrifice, and this final exhortation in the baptismal ceremony points the whole community to their accepted ministry, which is the sacrificial work of love and caring for the world.

The Ministry of Bishops

The rites for ordination in the Prayer Book changed little in the 1962 revision from those contained in the 1662 edition. In the *Book of Alternative Services* there is a new set of rites for all three orders, and though they articulate a similar understanding of ordained ministry to that of the Prayer Book, there are several amendments and additions which once again reflect the perspective of the post-Christendom church. These changes basically have to do firstly with recovering the place of the laos in the ordering of these ministries, and secondly with emphasizing the bishop's role as pastor and care-giver. Firstly, the ordination rites for all three orders provide for an affirmation by the community of God's call to an individual to his or her particular ministry. In doing this, the *Book of Alternative Services* attempts to recapture the biblical model of participation by the people in the raising up and authentication of persons entering holy orders.

The Prayer Book rites allowed only for objections to the proceedings by the people:

Yet if there be any of you who knoweth any impediment or notable crime in any of them, for the which he ought not to be received into this holy ministry; let him come forth in the Name of God, and show what the crime or impediment is.
(*BCP* p. 645)

But the *Book of Alternative Services* requires the more positive step of affirmation and a promise to uphold the person in his or her life and work:

Bishop	Is it your will that *N* be ordained a deacon (priest or bishop)?
People	It is.
Bishop	Will you uphold him/her in this ministry?
People	We will.

Interestingly, in the Prayer Book ordination of a bishop no provision for objection was made. The people could not refuse a bishop, where they could a deacon or priest. This is an example of how the Church of England rites were imported without proper adaptation to Canada. English bishops are appointed by the monarch and the people have no legal right of refusal, nor even of confirmation. Canadian bishops are elected by the clergy and laity of the diocese (or province), and the rite of episcopal ordination incorporates the affirmation by the diocese of that election.

The specific ministry to which a bishop is called is expressed succinctly in the World Council of Churches' document *Baptism, Eucharist and Ministry*:

Bishops preach the Word, preside at the sacraments, and administer discipline in such a way as to be representative pastoral

ministers of oversight, continuity and unity in the Church. They
have pastoral oversight of the area to which they are called.
They serve the apostolicity and unity of the Church's teaching,
worship and sacramental life. They have responsibility for
leadership in the Church's mission. They relate the Christian
community in their area to the wider Church, and the universal
Church to their community. They, in communion with the
presbyters and deacons and the whole community, are responsible for the orderly transfer of ministerial authority in the
Church.
(*BEM* p. 26–27)

This statement describes the main work of the bishop as oversight of the people (*episkope*) and leadership in both pastoral and
liturgical matters. Further, the bishop is called to be a symbol of the
intended unity of Christians. He unites the diocese with the universal church, and the contemporary community with the apostles.
Because he has inherited the ministry given to the apostles by our
Lord, the bishop has the responsibility of maintaining the faith and
teaching given by them to the church, and of ordering the ordained
ministry, whose authority is given to them by him through the laying on of hands. This agreed ecumenical summary of the nature of
episcopal ministry forms the basis of the service of the Ordination
of a Bishop in the *Book of Alternative Services*.
For example, one of the (three) ordaining bishops asks the
bishop-elect:

Bishop   As a chief priest and pastor, will you encourage and
support all baptized people in their gifts and ministries,
nourish them from the riches of God's grace, pray for
them without ceasing, and celebrate with them the
sacraments of our redemption?

Answer   I will, in the name of Christ, the shepherd and bishop of
our souls.
(*BAS* p. 637)

This is a new vow in the modern rite, and it reflects a changed
understanding of the word *pastor* in the post-Christendom context.
Where the Prayer Book clearly understands this to mean the main-
tainance of order, discipline, and the condemnation of error among

church members, the *Book of Alternative Services* recovers a gentler sense of the word, which means literally 'shepherd,' and invites the bishop to a supportive and encouraging ministry among the faithful, calling forth from them the gifts of the Spirit and praying for them constantly.

The responsibility for the good government of the church, historically the role of the bishops, is also expressed in the form of a vow:

Bishop Will you guard the faith, unity, and discipline of the Church?

Answer I will, for the love of God.

Bishop Will you share with your fellow bishops in the government of the whole Church; will you sustain your fellow presbyters and take counsel with them; will you guide and strengthen the deacons and all others who minister in the Church?

Answer I will, by the grace given me.
(*BAS* p. 637)

Again, there are new elements in these commitments which emphasize the shared nature of ministry rather than the exclusive power of bishops in the Christendom situation. While government and authority still rest unequivocally with the bishop in the new rites, the sense of the words is that they should be exercised in ways that reflect the servanthood of the chief pastor. He is to sustain the clergy and laity, and − another addition − to take counsel with them. The rite presumes that wisdom resides not simply in the leader but in the whole community, and the wise leader is the one who can draw it forth. A comparative glance at the Prayer Book will reveal that nothing in the older rite commits the bishop to consult with clergy or laity at all. Rather, the work of government is expressed very frequently as the duty to correct and punish the other members of the community for their failures. It has an altogether stern and schoolmasterly sound to it.

The pastoral nature of episcopal ministry in the *Book of Alternative Services* is further symbolized by the addition of the giving of a pastoral staff at the conclusion of the consecration. This act is a visible sign of the vow already made (like the ring in a wedding ceremony) by which the bishop has pledged himself to be the care-giver and nurturer of the church. The words spoken at this moment, the climax of the liturgy, remind the bishop of his duty to continue in the way of Christ, the Good Shepherd who laid down his life for his sheep:

> Receive this staff as a sign of your pastoral office; keep watch over the whole flock in which the Holy Spirit has appointed you to shepherd the Church of God. Encourage the faithful, restore the lost, build up the Body of Christ; that when the Chief Shepherd shall appear, you may receive the unfading crown of glory.
> (*BAS* p. 640)

The Ministry of Priests

The specific ministry to which a priest is called is also outlined succinctly in the WCC's *Baptism, Eucharist and Ministry:*

> Presbyters serve as pastoral ministers of word and sacraments in a local eucharistic community. They are preachers and teachers of the faith, exercise pastoral care, and bear responsibility for the discipline of the congregation to the end that the world may believe and that the entire membership of the Church may be renewed, strengthened, and equipped in ministry. Presbyters have particular responsibility for the preparation of members for Christian life and ministry.
> (*BEM* p. 27)

This statement singles out as the essence of priestly ministry the themes of pastoral care, preaching, and celebration, and the enabling of lay ministry. The priest is called to give the same nurture and leadership to the local community as is the bishop to the larger one. S/he is charged with the task of being both servant and leader, both responding to the needs of the people and at the same time challenging them to move forward in faith and action. The guiding purpose of his or her ministry is not to build up self, but to build up Christian community so that the community itself, rather than the priest alone, becomes a sign of hope and love to the surrounding society. This means that a priest is to be neither a social worker nor an ordained server, concerned exclusively with the world on the one hand or the sanctuary on the other, but is to be an example and teacher of the faith and an enabler of the worldly ministry of the people.

Such is the basis on which the rite of Ordination of a Priest in the *Book of Alternative Services* is written. There are significant differences in this liturgy from its equivalent in the Prayer Book, more so than in the rites for the other two orders. In fact, the 1662 service for the Ordering of Priests (unchanged in 1962) gives us a revealing glimpse into the condition of the clergy at the time of the Reformation, one which helps us understand some of the reasons for the relative ease with which the church as a whole accepted the change of government under the monarchy. Quite simply, the spiritual and intellectual condition of parish priests in England was generally appalling (Professor Dickens in his book *The English Reformation* suggests that the reason why there was not more opposition to the ending of the Pope's jurisdiction in England by the king is that the clergy didn't understand the arguments for or against it). Nothing reveals this better than the exhortation by the bishop to those about to be ordained to the priesthood in the old rite.

It is an extremely lengthy and severe exhortation, containing many warnings about the gravity of the office and weighty responsibility to which the candidates are to be admitted. Those persons who may be presuming to enter this holy order without due regard for its seriousness are threatened with "horrible punishment" by Christ on the day of judgement. It is too long to quote here, but look at this extract, and imagine what conditions in the church might prompt such a grave pronouncement:

Have always therefore printed in your remembrance, how great a treasure is committed to your charge. For they are the sheep of Christ, which he bought with his death, and for whom he shed his blood. The Church and the Congregation whom you must serve, is his spouse and his body. And if it shall happen the same Church, or any member thereof, to take any hurt or hindrance by reason of your negligence, ye know the greatness of the fault, and also the horrible punishment that will ensue. Wherefore consider with yourselves the end of your ministry toward the children of God, toward the spouse and body of Christ; and see that you never cease your labour, your care and diligence, until

you have done all that lieth in you, according to your bounden duty, to bring all such as are or shall be committed to your charge, unto that agreement in the faith and knowledge of God, and to that ripeness and perfectness of age in Christ, that there be no place left among you, either for error in religion, or for viciousness in life.
(BCP p. 649)

Glorious English, but ferocious words! One infers from this more than the usual despair of bishops for some of their clergy, but a genuine concern for the spiritual care of the church, which was obviously suffering after the years of corruption and laxity in pre-Reformation centuries that in part precipitated the desire for reform.

Contemporary Christians are, thankfully, much better served by their priests. The corruptions of the mediaeval church have been extirpated, and clergy today are carefully selected, trained, and supported in the work of parish ministry. As a result, the general spiritual condition of (those who remain in) the post-Christendom church may be much higher that the church of 400 years ago — though one must be cautious about such statements since, of course, we have no exact way of measuring the claim. At any rate, the *Book of Alternative Services* avoids any assumption of laxity or ignorance among those coming for ordination. The rites approach the candidates as worthy members of the church and adequately equipped for the high office and weighty responsibility to which they are called.

The new rite for the Ordination of a Priest begins with a prayer for the whole church (p. 644). This differs from the older rite, which began with a prayer for the candidates. It then continues with a shorter and more positive exhortation by the bishop outlining the duties and responsibilities of priesthood:

The Church is the family of God, the Body of Christ, and the temple of the Holy Spirit. All baptized people are called to make Christ known as Saviour and Lord, and to share in the renewing of his world. Now you are called to work as a pastor, priest, and teacher, together with your bishop and fellow presbyters, and to take your share in the councils of the Church.

As a priest it will be your task to proclaim by word and deed the gospel of Jesus Christ, and to fashion your life in accordance with its precepts. You are to love and serve the people among whom you work, caring alike for young and old, strong and weak, rich and poor. You are to preach, to declare God's forgiveness to penitent sinners, to pronounce God's blessing, to preside at the administration of holy baptism and at the celebration of the mysteries of Christ's body and blood, and to perform the other ministrations entrusted to you.

In all that you do, you are to nourish Christ's people from the riches of his grace, and strengthen them to glorify God in this life and in the life to come.
(*BAS* p. 646)

It is significant that this statement begins by recalling the ministry of the baptized. It thereby locates ordained priesthood within the royal priesthood of the laos. The vows which follow express the ministry of priest as a supportive and shared ministry, though the privilege of celebrating the sacraments and blessing and absolving the people is reserved to him or her and to the bishop. There is one particularly interesting difference in the new vows from the old, and it has to do with reading and study. In the *Book of Alternative Services* the priest is asked:

Will you be diligent in the reading and study of the holy scriptures, and in seeking the knowledge of such things as may make you a stronger and more able minister of Christ?
(*BAS* p. 647)

This question directs the priest to undertake a broad and systematic study (in other words, a program of continuing education) of sacred and secular subjects which will help in illuminating the gospel in his or her teaching ministry. The Prayer Book, however, betrays some rather more confining sentiments:

Will you be diligent in prayers, and in reading of the holy Scriptures, and in such studies as help in the knowledge of the same, laying aside the study of the world and the flesh?
(*BCP* p. 652)

The clergy in former days were only to read the Bible or commentaries on the Bible. They were not to stray into secular studies. Perhaps this indicates that their minds were secular enough already!

Two further variations in the new rite are worthy of note. First, the words of consecration themselves omit the reference, explicit in the Prayer Book, to the retention of sins. This is a puzzling omission, since the authority to withold absolution was given to the apostles by our Lord himself (see John 20: 23), and in certain rare instances may be a necessary pastoral device. The implication appears to be that the exercise of the right of retention is so rare that it need not be mentioned at all, but this deserves some re-examination by the authors.

Secondly, the closing act of the rite adds the giving of a chalice and paten — symbols of the eucharist — to the newly ordained person as a sign of the sacramental privilege bestowed upon her/him. This expands on the Prayer Book liturgy, which only provides for the giving of a Bible. The *Book of Alternative Services* includes the presentation of both a Bible and the eucharistic vessels, and in this way makes more complete the visible signs expressing the nature of the vows already made.

The Ministry of Deacons

Deacons represent to the Church its calling as servants in the world. By struggling in Christ's name with the myriad needs of societies and persons, deacons exemplify the interdependence of worship and service in the Church's life. They exercise responsibility in the worship of the congregation: for example by reading the scriptures, preaching and leading the people in prayer. They help in the teaching of the congregation. They exercise a ministry of love within the community. They fulfill certain administrative tasks and may be elected to responsibilities for governance.
(*BEM* p. 27)

Although the order of deacons in the church is older than that of priests, dating back to the time of the apostles (see Acts 6:1 - 6; also see chapter three), the role of deacons has been lost to a great degree in the church, their function being swallowed up by the higher orders. But now with the demise of its power and the privileges of empire, the church is recovering its diaconal role and discovering again the servant ministry of Christ among those who are thrust to the margins of society. With this has come a revival of the diaconate as a separate and distinct order of ministry.

In some parts of Canada men and women are being encouraged to enter the diaconate as a permanent commitment. This is the goal of their ministry, rather than priesthood. Instead of passing through the order in a temporary sojourn, these persons have discerned their vocation as a call to servanthood, and as a call to symbolize before the church and the world the servant ministry of all baptized persons. Their spiritual gifts are given for this end, rather than for the sacramental ministry of priesthood, and the church is gradually coming to accept and understand this ancient order, which it had forgotten was buried in the vaults of its own history.

Where it is being practised, the work of deacons is a ministry of seeking out the lonely and downcast, the marginalized and rejected, and bringing to them the comfort and strength of the gospel. It may be a ministry exclusively committed to the work of social justice, of working at the hard, practical side of our faith in the social, economic, and political issues of the day which require a response from Christians. Or it may be a ministry of pastoral care to the sick and the poor, or the encouragement of the unemployed and dependent, and so on. Wherever his or her place of work, the deacon is called to be a sign to the world outside the church of the compassion and the transforming power of Christ among those denied the fullness of life.

In the liturgy, the deacon is called to be a sign of the world's need among those who have already received the good news of life. Thus, his or her liturgical function includes the dismissal of the people at the end of the eucharist, sending them out in the name of the Lord to love and to serve. Also, the deacon traditionally receives the gifts of the community at the offertory, presenting them to the celebrant for offering up to God in thanksgiving. In this, s/he symbolizes the need of the community to give gifts to the Lord. Since God's own nature is to give, the deacon helps the community to become givers, to remember that we are first and foremost recipients of the Creator's grace and must return our thanks and tithes.

These liturgical functions along with the other principal diaconal privileges of reading the gospel and leading the prayers of the people, have been recovered and restored in the *Book of Alternative Services*. The rubrics guiding the enactment of the liturgy make clear which elements of it are to be led by the bishop, the priest, the deacons, or lay persons. Though these additions to the rites are clear enough, they will require some pointing out and teaching by the clergy for the people of today's church to understand their significance.

The Ordination of a Deacon in the *Book of Alternative Services* once again begins with a prayer for the whole church, and then moves on to a statement by the bishop outlining the principal ministry to which s/he is being ordered. Unlike the equivalent statement in the Prayer Book, which subordinates the deacons to the priests, the new rite makes it clear that they are to be assistants to the bishop, as was the case in the ancient world:

Every Christian is called to follow Jesus Christ, serving God the Father, through the power of the Holy Spirit. God now calls you to a special ministry of servanthood, directly under the authority of your bishop. In the name of Jesus Christ, you are to serve all people, particularly the poor, the weak, the sick, and the lonely.

As a deacon in the Church, you are to study the holy scriptures, to seek nourishment from them, and to model your life upon them. You are to make Christ and his redemptive love known, by your word and example, to those among whom you live and work and worship. You are to interpret to the Church the needs, concerns, and hopes of the world. You are to assist the bishop and priests in public worship, and in the ministration of God's word and sacraments, and you are to carry out other duties assigned to you from time to time. At all times, your life and teaching are to show Christ's people that in serving the helpless they are serving Christ himself.
(*BAS* p. 655)

The statement is designed to encompass the ordering of both transitional deacons, that is, those on their way to priesthood, and permanent deacons, those who will remain in this order as the goal of their ministry. Also, it is an exhortation intended for both the stipendiary and the non-stipendiary diaconate. Stipendiary deacons are those on the paid staff of a parish or other church community, while the latter are persons who have a vocation to servant ministry outside the professional structure of the church. These persons are ordered by the church for work and service in particular spheres of responsibility as an intentional witness to Christ beyond the church, but they are either unpaid for this work, or receive payment from some other salary source for other duties performed at the same time.

In these several ways, the *Book of Alternative Services* attempts to recover the variety of ministries which have always been a part of the church's life, but which have sometimes been obscured and diminished by the professional ministries of bishops and priests. The new rites affirm and uphold the gifts given by the Spirit to the whole people of God, but exercised differently according to the aptitudes and talents of particular individuals. They express all intentional Christian work and witness in its various forms as the exercise of ministry, and recall for us the fact that all ministry, both lay and ordained, is the consequence of baptism and is nothing less than the application in the world of our baptismal vows. If the million or so Anglicans in Canada ever come to see themselves as ministers of Christ, with particular gifts imparted to them by a deliberate grace, then the post-Christendom church in this country will become a dynamic force indeed: a light to lighten the (contemporary) Gentiles.

Questions for Discussion

1. What gifts for ministry exist in your group? List the gifts you see in the others around you now.
2. What kinds of ministry are happening in your church, other than ordained ministry? What else could happen if people got organized?
3. What do you see as the specific role of the ordained? Are there any ways in which the church does not allow them to function properly (e.g., by requiring them to do secretarial work, etc.)?

4. Most congregations don't know what the clergy are actually required to do. Ask your pastor to share with you the rewards and frustrations of his/her ministry, and to describe the range of clerical responsibilities.

7. Mission

Christians have discovered a new responsibility for the world, that loving their neighbours as themselves demands more than compliance with the civil law. As the letter of James puts it, it is not enough to say to the poor, 'Go in peace, be warmed and filled,' without giving them the things needed for the body" (2: 16). This finds expression in contemporary liturgy in consciousness of the ministry of Jesus to the distressed and in prayer for the extension of that justice which is God's own work. (from the introduction: *The Book of Alternative Services*)

A Missionary Church

According to the gospel of Matthew, the last words of the risen Christ to the disciples were: " 'Go forth, therefore, and make all nations my disciples; baptize men everywhere in the name of the Father and the Son and the Holy Spirit, and teach them to observe all that I have commanded you" (28: 19). These words have come to be known as the Great Commission, repeated with slight variations in both Mark (16: 15) and Luke (24: 27), and they have provided the impulse for mission by Christians throughout the centuries. All Christians are given the task of making Christ known and proclaiming the gospel of life by word and deed.

Anglicans have had a strong commitment to mission since our church began. Although our understanding of that mission has changed over the years, we have always understood ourselves to be a missionary people called together by God into community, gifted by the Spirit, and sent out into the world to make Christ's salvation known. Anglicanism has regarded mission as part of the essence of the church, an integral part of what we are called to be. Just as God sent his only Son into the world to bring us life, so God sends us into the world to make that life known through proclamation and action. The mission of the church, therefore, is an extension of the mission of Christ. Both gospel and world are destined for each other, and the church is called to be the agent which brings the two together in creative engagement. This means that the church, wherever it happens to be, is in a missionary situation.

Liturgy and Mission

The Prayer Book reflects a Christendom theology of mission. That is, it looks out upon the world from the perspective of the church's position at the centre of culture. From this vantage point, mission is seen as an activity from the centre to the periphery, as an expression of kindness by the haves to the have-nots, the giving out of spiritual and material bounty to those who possess neither. Its underlying conviction is what Dom Helder Camara, Roman Catholic bishop of Recife in Brazil, has called the *charity mentality*, that attitude which sees the poor as objects of pity rather than victims of injustice, and which sees the church as dispensing largesse rather than engaging in partnership with those it is called to serve.

It also reflects a Christendom perspective on evangelism. Since the Christendom church assumed the nation to be Christian, it placed little empahasis on evangelism at home. Evangelism was what the church did overseas, it was the purpose of its foreign mission. The domestic mission of the church was to provide schools, hospitals, poor houses, orphanages, and other social services which the state could not supply. Also, and most importantly, it was the mission of the church at home to uphold the Christian values of the culture, to keep the nation in church. Thus the rites in the old book stress the responsibility of Christians to care for the less fortunate, to pray for the salvation of the heathen, and to uphold the social order. It was taken for granted that the social order was the most benefical for the less fortunate, and that the non-Christian world was just waiting for the church.

Post-Christendom, however, has generated some new perspectives on mission. The church finds itself no longer at the centre of culture or the political structures of the state. The latter has taken over most of the social services which once formed the bulk of the church's domestic mission. Overseas churches, though mostly not yet self-supporting, are autonomous and growing and can often provide more expertise in evanglism and church growth than their founders. The secularization of culture and subsequent decline in religious commitment has placed the church in a minority situation, facing the task of domestic evangelism on a large scale for the first time since the pre-Constantinian era. And the growth of ecumenical co-operation, particularly where this has called for a prophetic stance toward established authorities, has produced a new political awareness which is forcing many Anglicans out of their former uncritical acceptance of state religion.

The post-Christendom church is beginning to view its mission no longer from the perspective of the centre, but from the position of people who live on the periphery. Mission today is being expressed in terms of a new sensitivity to those who are at the margins and edges of the social order. Christians are coming to understand how political power is experienced by the powerless, and are learning how those at the margins can minister to and with each other as partners in a common cause. Servanthood, or *diakonia,* is coming to mean more than caring for the less fortunate, but seeking justice for the vicitims and making peace among the powerful. Prophesy is coming to mean more than the denunciation of sin in individuals, but the exposing of corporate, social evil and systemic injustice. There is a new awareness of the mutuality of mission, the spiritual and material resources we need to receive as well as those we have to give. As we experience more of life on the margins we are discovering something of the richness of the poor, and the poverty of our own earlier wealth. Anglicans still understand themselves as sent in mission (for the most part), but the nature of that mission is significantly different from that expressed in the Prayer Book.

The *Book of Alternative Services* reflects this post-Christendom perspective on mission, therefore. It expresses a theology of mission for a church which finds itself in a variety of different relationships with both political authority and with other religious bodies throughout the world. The place of the church in society is no longer limited to that of charity, but is expressed in the new rites in terms of a commitment to peace-making, justice, and the creation of social structures which uphold rather than diminish personal and communal freedom. The narrow nationalism of the earlier concept of mission gives way now to a broader vision of global community, transcending the interests of secular principalities and powers.

Christians are called into partnership with all people who are working for a just, participatory, and sustainable society. The evangelism that is presented stresses a personal faithfulness to Christ which transcends national loyalties and may sometimes lead Christians to challenge human authorities.

Let's take a look at some specific examples. First, the prophetic mission of the church.

Prophetic Mission

The Reformation and its aftermath precipitated a long period of instability in England, resulting in civil and religious wars, insurrections, succession crises, and the threat of external invasion. Owing its well-being to the Crown, the church was co-opted early on in the task of maintaining social stabilty and domestic peace. Good citizenship features in the Prayer Book as an expression of Christian virtue. Criminals and evil-doers are villified and the duty of magistrates to punish them severely is repeatedly upheld. The compassion of our Lord for prostitutes and sinners became strangely obscured in this era of church-state interdependence, as the mission of Christians was rendered increasingly inseparable from national goals.

As we have already seen, the *Book of Alternative Services* expresses the changed nature of church-state relationship in the modern period (see chapter two). Moving beyond state religion, the new ties remind us of that Jesus who upheld the cause of the marginalized over that of the powerful. Whether the powerful were individuals or institutions, Jesus displayed a preferential option for the poor whenever their interests came into conflict. This prophetic mood is well expressed in the new rites, for example, in the prayer at the conclusion of the service of the Blessing of Oil:

Lord God,
in baptism you anoint us with your Holy Spirit,
and in this eucharist you feed us with the bread of life.
Strengthen us in our ministry of service
that we may preach good news to the poor,
proclaim release to the captives
and recovery of sight to the blind,

set at liberty those who are oppressed,
and proclaim the acceptable year of the Lord.
(*BAS* p. 622)

The words of this prayer echo Jesus' first sermon in the
synagogue at Nazareth (see Luke 4:16–20) in which he declared
God's compassion for those whom the world customarily ignores.
There is more than a simply pastoral sentiment in the prayer. It incorporates us symbolically into the declaration made in the
Nazareth sermon. It asks for strength to engage in the prophetic
work of Christ in a ministry of solidarity and witness with those
who are not at the centre. It is a prayer which identifies Christians
with the poor, the prisoners, the blind, and the oppressed rather
than merely expressing concern for them. It goes beyond the
Christendom assumption that the weak must wait upon the strong
for justice, and expresses the hope that God will act on behalf of the
weak so that they may gain justice for themselves. And the prayer
summons the church to be in partnership with them in this
endeavour.

The same summons is repeated in the propers (i.e., appropriate
prayers) for Holy Innocents' Day:

Merciful God,
accept all we offer you this day.
Preserve your people from cruelty
and indifference to violence,
that the weak may always be defended
from the tyranny of the strong.
(*BAS* p. 398)

The theme of innocent suffering in the *Book of Alternative
Sevices*, largely absent from the Prayer Book except in reference to
our Lord, reflects the experience of millions of people who live in
situations of poverty, disease, war, and state brutality all over the
world. These people are more sinned against than sinning (to borrow Shakespeare's phrase), more the victims of inhumanity and injustice than its perpetrators. Refugees, the homeless, the victims of
racism and religious intolerance, aboriginal peoples, the handicapped — people by the millions who suffer not merely from cir-

cumstance but from man-made policies and structures which disregard human rights and dignity. These are the ones whom the prayer asks to be preserved. It also summons the comfortable out of their indifference to this cruelty and urges them to defend all human dignity and innocence as they would their own.

Justice

The prophetic mission of the church is linked in the new rites to the theme of justice, a recurrent theme throughout both the Prayer Book and the *Book of Alternative Services.* In the New Testament the word for justice is *dikaiosoune.* Older biblical translations render this as *righteousness,* but it comes from the same root as the word *dike* which means "judge," one who dispenses justice, and therefore includes the idea of righting wrongs and establishing just relationships. Newer biblical translations render this no longer as *righteousness,* which has come to connote a merely individual moral uprightness, but rather as *justice,* which captures the fullness of the biblical idea. God's justice is both an individual morality and the establishment of social relationships free from dominance and dependency. The new rites, particularly in the litanies and intercessions, try to capture this personal/social duality of justice in its scriptural depth.

> Cleanse our hearts of prejudice and selfishness, and inspire us to hunger and thirst for what is right.
> Lord, hear our prayer.
> (*BAS* p. 112)

> We pray to be forgiven our sins and set free from all hardship, distress, want, war, and injustice.
> Lord, hear and have mercy.
> (*BAS* p. 114)

> Assist your people in every land, govern them in peace and justice, defend them from the enemies of life; O Lord, hear our prayer;
> Kyrie eleison.
> (*BAS* p. 117)

These prayers suggest that hardship, want, and human distress are more than a result of misfortune and bad luck. In a world where there is more than enough food, wealth, and technology to provide for everyone, the persistence of poverty and hunger is a deliberate act of human sinfulness. It is a consequence of human will, not of economic calamity. Mission, therefore, is no longer a matter of dispensing charity. It is about changing man-made structures and policies that ensure the perpetuation of this sin. This involves creating among Christian people a new attitude to law and lawmakers. Justice and law are not always the same thing (as many in South Africa and elsewhere can attest). Where the Prayer Book urged conformity with the law and with the legally established powers, the *Book of Alternative Services* points the church to those who are victims of unjust law, used as a weapon of terror, and to the lawlessness of governments. It encourages those of us who do not experience these things to stand in solidarity with those who have been persecuted for seeking God's justice and equity:

Hear our prayers for all our sisters and brothers in faith
who suffer for truth, justice, and freedom.
Strengthen their witness
and keep them, with us,
under the protection of your wings.
(*BAS* p. 418)

This prayer (to be said after communion on Saint Stephen's Day, the commemoration of the first Christian martyr) recognizes that it is the experience of many still to suffer for the cause of right. The *Book of Alternative Services* includes a number of prayers for these persons, victims on account of their prophetic conscience:

Strengthen those who suffer for the sake of conscience. When they are accused, save them from speaking in hate; when they are rejected, save them from bitterness; when they are imprisoned, save them from despair. Give us grace to discern the truth, that our society may be cleansed and strengthened.
(*BAS* p. 681)

And again:

> Let us pray for all who are condemned to exile, prison, harsh
> treatment, or hard labour, for the sake of justice and truth: the
> Lord support them and keep them steadfast.
> Lord hear our prayer.
> (*BAS* p. 115)

> For the whole human family, that we may live together in justice
> and peace, let us pray to the Lord.
> Lord, have mercy.
> (*BAS* p. 116)

These prayers and litanies are clearly global in scope. They express no political bias towards the right or the left, condemning
some regimes and ignoring the brutality of others, as some claim
the church is wont to do. They point, rather to the sad and sorry
universality of human cruelty and viciousness in the face of
legitimate opposition and dissent, and remind us that out Lord
himself was the victim of such injustice by the powerful, a reality
which has increased in the modern world with its obscene
militarization of rich and poor nations alike, and the paranoia of
the national security state among politicians throughout the world.
They pray for steadfast courage and continuing witness among
those who take a prophetic stance in opposition to these values of
death.

Also, we find in the new rites a focus on the sharing of global
resources. As rich Christians in a world of hunger, we need to be
reminded of our responsibility to those who are excluded from fair
access to the world's food, technology, and wealth. We live now in
a world of increasing economic and political interdependence,
where the opportunities for the building up of human community
on a broad scale are vast and urgent. In the twentieth century, the
church has recognized that its mission can no longer be confined to
domestic or national interests alone, but is inextricably linked with
the interests of the international community as a whole. In the
Book of Alternative Services, therefore, we are called to envisage a
global community where all may enjoy the fruits of the creation
equitably and peacefully. We meet a new focus on interna-

tionalism, a vision of worldwide community in which there is a commitment to justice and to the sharing of resources:

> May we discover new and just ways of sharing the goods of the earth, struggling against exploitation, greed, or lack of concern:
> May we all live by the abundance of your mercies and find joy together:
> Lord, hear and have mercy.
> (*BAS* p. 114)

> Give to all nations an awareness of the unity of the human family.
> Lord, hear our prayer.
> (*BAS* p. 112)

> Teach us to use your creation for your greater praise, that all may share the good things you provide.
> Lord, hear our prayer.
> (*BAS* p. 112)

This internationalism stands in marked contrast to the sometimes uncritical nationalism of the Prayer Book. It moves us beyond local, cultural, and racial limitations to embrace a wider vision of global community, one united and reconciled in mutual respect and equality of justice. It is this vision, with its roots in the teaching and example of Christ, which is the basis of the church's prophetic mission in the *Book of Alternative Services*.

Peace-Making

Closely associated with the search for global justice is the mission of peace-making. Ours is the first generation in history to possess the capacity to end life on the planet. We can now undo in minutes what God has fashioned over millennia. The very real threat of nuclear extinction, along with the increasing dangers of global poverty and oppression, have created a new consciousness among Christians of the importance of peace-making and of the urgency of ending the traditional hostilities and mutual suspicions which have divided people in all nations throughout history. Although this is an area of concern which Christians share with men and women of many other ideologies and faiths, the church's call to the mission of peace-making comes directly from our Lord himself:

> Blessed are the peace-makers; for they shall be called the children of God. (Matthew 5: 9)

The nuance of this statement has often been missed. Jesus directed the words at the peace-makers, not the peace-lovers. This implies a responsibility among Christians to engage actively in the search for peace and reconciliation, rather than merely to seek a passive tranquility and stillness within. Both, of course, are desirable, but one without the other is an incomplete expression of the fullness of Christ's peace which he promised to all who would take up his cross. In fact, the scriptures contain over 350 references to peace, indicating that it has been a central dimension of the religious agenda throughout history.

Peace is not a new liturgical discovery, of course. It is an element in the Prayer Book, found in many places. But there it is presented largely in terms of a summons to personal righteousness and the avoidance of social strife and violence, and the containment of religious and political heresy. This emphasis on personal morality is an essential element in any full understanding of the peace which God intends for humanity. But the Prayer Book has a tendency to *spiritualize* peace, to make it primarily an interior quality. See, for instance, the collect for Holy Innocents' Day:

> O Almighty God, who out of the mouths of babes and sucklings hast ordained strength, and madest infants to glorify thee by their deaths; mortify and kill all vices in us, and so strengthen us by thy grace, that by the innocency of our lives, and constancy of our faith even unto death, we may glorify thy holy Name. (*BCP* p. 111)

The event which the prayer commemorates, of course, is the slaughter of innocent children by King Herod shortly after our Lord's birth. The spiritualizing of this event in the Prayer Book turns it into an occasion for reflection upon our inward personal vices, and a request for strength to retain our moral constancy in the face of our own suffering and death. To the modern ear, however, this seems an incomplete petition. Peace is not merely internal tranquility. The widespread violations of human rights in many societies, and the sensitivity which many Christians have to the rights of the unborn, reminds us that death of innocent life is still very much part of the world's injustice. God's redemption of the world is not merely an interior redemption of individual hearts, but, in the biblical view, includes the transformation of the political and economic conditions which give rise to such wrong–doing. The collect as it appears in the *Book of Alternative Services*, therefore, contains a petition for the concrete transformation of human community so that the innocent may suffer no more:

> Almighty God, our heavenly Father, whose children suffered at the hands of Herod, receive, we pray, all innocent victims into the arms of your mercy. By your great might frustrate all evil designs and establish your reign of justice, love, and peace.
> (*BAS* p. 398)

Other prayers and petitions take up the church's commitment to justice and peace-making in its worldwide mission:

> For the peace of the whole world, for the welfare of the holy Church of God, and for the unity of all, let us pray to the Lord.
> Lord, have mercy.
> (*BAS* p. 110)

> Let us pray for the peace of the world: the Lord grant that we may live together in justice and faith.
> Lord, hear our prayer.
> (*BAS* p. 114)

> Let us ask the Lord for peace and justice in the world.
> Lord, have mercy.
> (*BAS* p. 118)

The linking of peace and justice is an important development in the new rites. To pray for peace without recognizing that the cause of so much hostility and violence lies in those attitudes and structures which deny many people the hope of sharing in the world's bounty and the freedom to make decisions about their own lives, is to pray only for the continuance of the status quo. Peace without change is a hopeless prospect for the majority of the world's people. At the same time, the pursuit of justice ruthlessly and without any compassion offers no greater prospect of equity and global security. Both mercy and equality are implied in these prayers, which always avoid the danger of seeking one without the other from a God who has demonstrated both peace-making and justice-building, both mercy and judgement, in the incarnate Christ.

The integral reality of peace as both personal and social harmony, both interior tranquility and global transformation, is well captured in the social prayer for peace which is found in the Occasional Prayers:

> O God, it is your will to hold both heaven and earth in a single peace. Let the design of your great love shine on the waste of our wraths and sorrows, and give peace to your Church, peace among nations, peace in our homes, and peace in our hearts. (*BAS* p. 677)

This beautifully crafted prayer conjures up a vision of all life and creation permeated by a single and unbroken web of love. Just as the light of God's radiance penetrates every corner of the universe from the smallest part to the greatest, so the prayer expresses the hope that peace may some day reign in every dimension of human existence, from the heart to the home, within the church, and throughout the international community. It gathers together many of the themes we are discussing, which are woven into the fabric of the new rites in interlocking ways, of Christian unity, global community, justice, and personal discipleship. The interrelatedness of all things, which is essentially a spiritual rather than an historical claim, is a vision especially necessary for a missionary church in a dangerously polarized age.

Diakonia

Throughout the *Book of Alternative Services* we encounter an understanding of mission as *diakonia* or servanthood. Christians are called through baptism and worship to serve the world as Christ came to serve. There are, accordingly, fewer aggressive and military images of the church in the language of the new services, no prayers for the church "militant here in earth." We find an absence of the triumphalism which marked the church's understanding of itself and its mission during the era of Christendom. Rather, the contemporary rites express a new sense of limitation and a more apostolic concept of service in the church's relationship with the world. See, for instance, the collect for proper 14:

> Almighty God, your Son Jesus Christ has taught us that what we do for the least of your children we do also for him. Give us the will to serve others as he was the servant of all, who gave up his life and died for us.
> (*BAS* p. 366)

This prayer is based on the parable of the sheep and the goats in Matthew 25. It recalls the judgement that will come upon the nations which ignore the cries of the distressed. The image of mission it suggests is that of servanthood. As our Lord taught us to serve him in the least of all his children, so the prayer asks for such a spirit of caring and commitment in the church, that we may carry out his command. The prayers over the gifts for this Sunday continue the theme of the day:

> God of heaven and earth, receive our sacrifice of praise, and strengthen us for the perfect freedom of your service.

As does the prayer after communion:

> O God, may we who have shared in holy things never fail to serve you in your world, and so come to the fullness of joy.

Every celebration of the eucharist ends with the dismissal:

> Leader Go in peace to love and serve the Lord.
> People Thanks be to God.

The rite for Maundy Thursday is a particularly powerful expression of the diaconal mission of Christians. It provides for the washing of feet in a ritual re-enactment of the event at the Last Supper, recorded in the New Testament. The symbolism of this liturgy, which begins the sacred three-day celebration of our Lord's passion, suggests that the mission of the church is portrayed in Jesus' act of bathing and cleansing the feet of his disciples. The liturgical re-enactment of this act of lowly service (which is optional and not mandatory in the *Book of Alternative Services*) may follow the reading of the Maundy Thursday gospel. Representatives of the congregation are invited to come forward, and the celebrant — usually the priest or deacon — explains the significance of the ritual in these words:

> Fellow servants of our Lord Jesus Christ,
> on the night before his death,
> Jesus set an example for his disciples
> by washing their feet, an act of humble service.
> He taught that strength and growth
> in the life of the kingdom of God
> come not by power, authority, or even miracle,
> but by such lowly service.
>
> Therefore, I invite you
> (who have been appointed as representatives
> of the congregation and)
> who share in the royal priesthood of Christ,
> to come forward,
> that I may recall whose servant I am
> by following the example of my Master.
> But come remembering his admonition
> that what will be done for you
> is also to be done by you to others,
> for "a servant is not greater than his master,
> nor is one who is sent greater than the one who sent him.
> If you know these things, blessed are you if you do them."
> (*BAS* p. 305)

Of all the new additions to the liturgy of our church, this is going to be the hardest for many of us to accept. Baring our feet in the sanctuary and having them washed by the rector will require a lot of courage and humility among Anglicans — as it did among the disciples. But Jesus knew precisely what the disciples needed to learn before they could become effective missionaries of the gospel. They had to overcome their fear of serving. They had to be freed from their fear of lowliness, of losing their dignity in the world.

The hardest task for post-Christendom Christians will be, I suspect, the discovery of this inward and spiritual liberation from the fear of indignity after the loss of power and cultural prestige. It does not come easily to those accustomed to the trappings of privilege. Yet it is the way the new rites call us to go. We are to discover the meaning of that lovely Prayer Book phrase "whose service is perfect freedom" in our mission and ministry in the world. An important dimension of that discovery will be the ability to receive as well as to give. Christians, especially those of us in the Western world, need to learn what we lack as well as what we possess, and what other Christians can give us, as well as what they need from us. Moving from the centre to the periphery, from a Ptolemaic theology of mission to a shared theology of mission, has changed our concept of service and fellowship. Mission in the new rites is about receiving as well as giving, about partnership as well as leadership, and the words of invitation in this Maundy Thursday liturgy are intended to open up our imaginations to the implications of this fundamental theological and cultural shift.

Evangelism

Mission and evangelism are distinct — though related — activities. Mission is the work of creating a social order in which men and women may live in peace with justice, and thus discover the conditions in which the fullness of life may be enjoyed in both its material and spiritual dimensions. Evangelism is the work of bringing individuals to a personal knowledge of Christ's saving love and forgiveness. It is, as the word itself suggests, a sharing of the *evangel*, the good news of Christ. In post-Christendom, where Christian ideas and values no longer permeate the culture uniformly, evangelism needs to receive new attention from Anglicans. We are in a cultural marketplace, a pluralistic society in which Christianity must compete with other systems of belief and value for a hearing by the people. Just as the apostle Paul had to go out into places where people gathered and where the scholars debated in order to preach the gospel, so the church today must come out of its buildings and go into the centres of public debate and activity where the great issues of human life are discussed.

In particular, evangelism needs to be rescued from its present Babylonian captivity by narrow, fundamentalist sects. So-called TV evangelists have given Christianity a bad name among great sections of our population who, having no connection with the church, possess no biblical or theological understanding with which to judge their message or method. Both the content and style of these purveyors of media religion have little in common with the catholic tradition of Christian faith. Their preoccupation seems to be with growth, expansion, and financial self-aggrandizement. These goals of size, bigness, success, and the accumulation of political clout arise more from the (worst) values of American culture than from the life of the poor man of Nazareth. In fact, it is ironic that, just as the mainstream of the church is discovering the richness of its poverty, the extreme margins of the church — with a mixture of cultural retrenchment and historical amnesia — are busily re-inventing Christendom.

Anglicans and other Christians blessed with a longer memory are now faced with the task of discovering an authentic evangelism that is faithful to the example of Jesus, and yet is effective in communicating the gospel in a media-oriented society. This will be no easy task, but it cannot be avoided by those who live under the commandment of our Lord's Great Commission, and it must not be abandoned to clever and manipulative religious salesmen who seem more often to be communicating the bad news of elitism, expansionism, and nationalism rather than the good news of God's unconditional love.

Whatever that authentic evangelism may be, it will be a personal evangelism. The sharing of inward discoveries and spiritual wealth between one soul and another is above all an activity that requires persons to be in relationship with each other. Impersonal forms of evangelism — such as television necessarily imposes, and much street preaching seems to involve — cannot be either a faithful reflection of the ministry of Jesus, nor in the end an effective means of incorporating individuals into the body of Christ. Veteran Anglican evangelist John Stott argues persuasively now for what he calls "fellowship evangelism," which is that deep sharing of personal knowledge of Jesus Christ in situations where there can be a dialogue of mutual listening. Genuine evangelism involves more listening than speaking, or else it is nothing more than a one-way harangue.

Two Styles of Evangelism

In the history of our church there have been two types of evangelism. We might describe these as the evangelism of *attraction* and the evangelism of *outreach*. Both have an important place in the liturgical tradition of Anglicanism, though in different times and places each has received varying emphasis.

1. Attraction Evangelism. Throughout the greater part of Christendom (and, indeed, of post-Christendom) Anglicans have relied upon attraction as the primary method of reaching the unreached. Through the establishment of a central place in the community, through the acquisition of influence and power in public affairs, and in the creation of beautiful worship designed to draw people to God, we have been very successful in making Christ visible and attractive to millions of men and women throughout the world. Perhaps our most cherished instrument of attraction, at least among Anglicans themselves, has been the liturgy.

Reverent and dignified worship is intrinsically appealing to the human soul. This is the insight from the tradition of liturgical spirituality which the compilers of Anglican worship have brilliantly preserved. Beautiful prayer and splendid ceremony can be a vehicle of divine grace and provide the moment for human encounter with the Source of all beauty and life. In the liturgy it is possible to transcend time and space and enter the very courts of heaven in praise and thanksgiving. So powerful is the human yearning for transcendence and fulfilment that Anglicans have often felt that they had to do little more than provide occasions for rich and satisfying public worship. Like a monastery set on a hill towards which people stream without being bidden, so our worship has acted as a beacon calling men and women to God's light. There have been times, past and present, when this alone was considered enough.

2. Outreach Evangelism. Anglicans are, for the most part, already familiar with the first kind of evangelism. Not so familiar is the outreach type, that is, going beyond the walls of the church to seek out those who do not yet know their need of God or who yearn for a fuller life. For most of us this is an uncomfortable area of Christian witness. The Jehovah's Witness model immediately occurs to many Anglicans. But this is not the fellowship or diaconal model of which our new worship is speaking. In most parishes it is possible to find men and women who are gifted and eager to undertake hospital and nursing-home visiting, for example. With proper training, teams of pastoral care volunteers can be of great service to the sick and shut-in, bringing them the assurance of the local church's concern and prayers. Obviously, the purpose of such visits is not to moralize, preach, or convert, but to demonstrate Christ's compassion for the sufferer and to offer support and comfort. The pastoral visitor is an ambassador for the God who heals.

Neighbourhood groups or house churches — when connected with the local church and its worshipping members — are an excellent method of evangelistic outreach. People who would not normally accept an invitation to a Sunday service will often be willing to accept an invitation to a neighbour's home to meet some members of the church. These events can be largely social, but should include some opportunity for religious conversation without browbeating or harassing the newcomer. The Anglican Church of Canada produces some good, short videotapes for just this purpose, since television is an almost universal medium in our society. A short discussion on some contemporary issue after viewing a videotape in a neighbour's front room can be the first introduction to Christian faith for many people. My experience is that many non-religious people often find this enjoyable and quite unpressured. It dissolves the myths and stereotypes that many of them carry around about Christians. They are led to discover that they have been staying away from something which does not really exist, and that the real thing — namely, a vital Christian community — can be very stimulating.

Many parishes are now offering training to members on how to witness to Christ in the workplace or at school. Again, this has nothing to do with nailing people at their desk or workbench with "Are you saved?" questions, but showing Christians how to stand up for themselves in debate, how to maintain a Christian perspective in difficult decisions of the marketplace, how to confront effectively anti-religious statements or racial slurs. Most Bible study groups and adult Christian-education programs are intended to equip church members to swim against the tide of a religiously indifferent society and to recover their nerve in maintaining a public faith.

Liturgy and Evangelism

Both these styles of evangelism are encouraged in the *Book of Alternative Services*. Our tradition of beautiful and dignified worship is continued in the careful construction of the new rites, which can be celebrated with all the reverence and dignity of the older services. Indeed, as we have seen, the contemporary liturgies have been enriched by the addition of many new prayers and canticles, litanies, and intercessions, all of which are intended to enhance the rich spiritual content of Anglican worship. People seeking a deeper knowledge of God will continue to be drawn to the church by modern services, just as they were by the traditional ones. But unlike in the traditional ones, they will be encouraged in the new services to take this knowledge of God out again into the world in evangelistic outreach.

The new liturgies go further than the former ones in urging Christians to show the love of Christ to those who have yet no understanding of it. The Good Friday liturgy, for instance, contains this prayer:

Merciful God,
Creator of the peoples of the earth and lover of souls,
have compassion on all who do not know you
as you are revealed in your Son Jesus Christ.
Let your gospel be preached with grace and power
to those who have not heard it,
turn the hearts of those who resist it,
and bring home to your fold those who have gone astray,
that there may be one flock and one shepherd. . . .
(*BAS* p.312)

In the context of the Good Friday service, these words point us to the universal purpose of Christ's sacrifice on the cross, and to the redemption of the whole world which was begun there. This event, which found its fulfilment in the resurrection on Easter Day, forms the basis of the Church's proclamation of the gospel to all peoples. It is the responsibility of all individual Christians to make this gospel known. Evangelism is the duty of every member of the church. This is made clear in the eucharistic rite, for example, which ends with a prayer that sends the faithful out into the world to witness courageously to Christ:

> May we, who share his body,
> live his risen life;
> we, who drink his cup,
> bring life to others;
> we, whom the Spirit lights,
> give light to the world.
> Keep us firm in the hope you have set before us,
> so that we and all your children shall be free,
> and the whole earth live to praise your name. . . .
> (*BAS* p.214)

The thrust of this prayer of thanksgiving after communion is to remind us that the gospel is not the private possession of Christians, to be guarded and admired like an object in a museum. It is a gift to the whole world, entrusted to us for proclamation by word and deed. That is one of the undertakings we make at baptism. The new baptismal rite contains this question:

> Celebrant Will you proclaim by word and example the good
> news of God in Christ?
> People   I will, with God's help.
> (*BAS* p.159)

And later, in the same service of baptism, at the giving of the light, we hear the exhortation:

> Let your light so shine before others
> that they may see your good works
> and glorify your Father in heaven.
> (*BAS* p.160)

We are to shine as lights in the world, testifying by the quality of our lives to the saving love and forgiveness of Christ. This statement manages to unify both outreach and attraction into a single, comprehensive image. By the radiance of our faith, and by our diaconal works, we are to be living vessels of the gospel in the world. Each of us, at baptism, becomes an evangelist.

There are many further examples. The collect for one of the Sundays in September (proper 24) expresses the evangelistic prayer:

Almighty God,
you call your Church to witness
that in Christ we are reconciled to you.
Help us so to proclaim the good news of your love,
that all who hear it may turn to you.
(*BAS* p.380)

This prayer focuses on the evangelism of love. This is one of the most overused words in post-Christendom. Love does not mean any sentimental emotion, any warm feeling in the heart. Love is a commitment, a decision to seek the good of the other whatever it may cost. Often enough, it is a painful commitment, the very opposite of sentimentality and good feelings, in short, a cross. It is this Christ-like love to which the prayer refers. Just as our Lord loved the world unto death, so the church and its members are to dwell in that love and to live it out in our personal and social relationships. This costly discipleship is not a summons to martyrdom, but to a very practical and unselfish commitment to the well-being of all God's people. Christian love is the greatest of all the tools of evangelism.

The thought is continued in other places. The rite for Ministry to the Sick is designed to offer victims of pain and sickness the assurance of God's healing presence. This service (see pages 551 – 558) continues the practice established already in the Prayer Book of creating a liturgical opportunity for sharing the gospel with people in situations of illness or imminent death. The assurance of pardon and the laying on of hands are central aspects of this service, which can be led by both lay and ordained members of the community. A bishop, if present, or priest, or authorized lay person may anoint the person with the words:

As you are outwardly anointed with this holy oil,
so may our heavenly Father grant you
the inward anointing of the Holy Spirit.
Of his great mercy,
may he forgive you your sins,
release you from suffering,
and restore you to wholeness and strength.
May he deliver you from all evil,
preserve you in all goodness,
and bring you to everlasting life.
(*BAS* p.555)

Once again, the evangelism expressed in these rites is one of personal concern and diaconal love, a showing forth of Christ in the way Christ himself lived and taught. This is very far from the conquest evangelism, with its insensitive hectoring and impersonal aggressiveness. It does not confuse evangelism with membership drives. The recruitment of church members is a legitimate and necessary activity, but evangelism is a much broader one. Its goal is not the filling of pews, but the conversion of those who do not already possess a saving faith to the saving power of Christ.

Preaching

Within the liturgy itself, the primary evangelistic event is the homily or sermon. Good preaching is always a matter of taste, and Anglicans rarely agree on what constitutes a good sermon, but you know one when you hear one. Ideally, a sermon should be both *pastoral* and *prophetic*. It should offer reassurance to its hearers of the good news of God's love and forgiveness, and should stir up the faithful to courageous witness and action in the world. The old preacher's saw is that s/he is called to comfort the disturbed and to disturb the comfortable.

From its very beginning, the Anglican church has insisted on the preaching of God's word as an integral and indispensable part of Christian public worship. From the late Middle Ages up to the Reformation, preaching was a sporadic and intermittent event in church life. The general level of education of parish clergy, other than the senior incumbents, was poor, and a great many ordained priests and monks were functionally illiterate. "Mass priests" were a common sight — men trained to memorize the liturgy and celebrate the eucharist by rote and with great frequency, but not to preach. Often they were employed by wealthy patrons to offer masses for the dead in the belief that this would aid the onward journey of the deceased in the afterlife. This is the origin of the small chapels called *chantries* still visible in the British Isles.

The English Reformation eventually brought an end to the inadequate training of clergy and the impoverished spirituality of the laity. The first Prayer Books established the liturgical unity of word and sacrament. The celebration of the eucharist was to include a homily on the scripture readings for the day. The faithful were to be nourished both in soul and mind, that is, by the hearing of God's word and the receiving of the sacrament of grace. This liturgical unity, a hallmark of Anglicanism, is continued in the *Book of Alternative Services*. Every celebration of the eucharist, whether on Sunday or midweek, whether in the early morning or in the mid-morning, is to include an exposition of the scriptures for the day (see the instructions on page 175).

The three-year ecumenical lectionary is intended to be the basis for preaching in the liturgy. It has been constructed so that the three lections given for the day are linked together by a common theme, the exposition of which will be spiritually profitable for the hearers. This theme can usually be discerned in both the Old Testament reading and the gospel. The epistle is usually independent of the other two lections, following a separate pattern of reading allowing major portions of the New Testament letters to be read sequentially week after week.

The value of lectionary preaching is twofold. Firstly, it is intended to unfold the scriptures to the people of God. In a biblically illiterate age, this is important since the misuse of scripture is almost as widespread as the ignorance of scripture. The mere hearing of lessons read out in church is not sufficient to convey understanding, and so the homily — which, in the new rites, comes immediately after the lessons — is intended to expound their meaning in such a way that the people of God may be nourished and strengthened for the work of ministry and witness. The *Book of Alternative Services* suggests that preaching (like liturgy itself) should always be contextual. "It is the application of the word of

God to the pastoral needs of a particular community at a particular time and place" (p.175).

Secondly, lectionary preaching imposes a healthy discipline upon the preacher. Expounding scripture in a contextual way requires him or her to know both the congregation and the texts. This involves considerable maturity and spiritual understanding on the part of the one given the responsibility, and cannot be done without adequate prayer and time for preparatory study. Parishes which allow their clergy no time for reading and reflection do themselves, as well as their pastors, no service. Bad preachers need even more time, and should be even less burdened with unnecessary duties. Lectionary preaching is intended to free the congregation from the tyranny of the preacher's hobbyhorse — the weekly repetition of favourite ideas ad nauseam — and imposes instead the discipline of expounding the whole of the gospel from the whole of scripture. Properly done, it prevents idiosyncratic selectivity and promotes comprehensive teaching.

When this happens, the sermon becomes an evangelistic event. Conversion is, after all, the result of an encounter between a yearning heart and the word of Life. Empty hearts can be filled by many things, but few things truly satisfy. The great privilege of the preacher is that s/he has been given words to speak which are words of eternal life (see John 6: 68) and spiritual food to give out such that whoever receives it shall never hunger again. What an immense gift this is! How sad when it is wasted on verbal dissertations or extempore ramblings which increase rather than satisfy spiritual hunger.

Evangelism and Other Religions

The Christendom church had a habit of gazing out upon the world and dividing humanity into two categories, the saved and the damned. Theologians, of course, would quibble about where the line between them was to be drawn. The Council of Trent, a massive rallying point for the Roman Catholic church after the Reformation, drew the line around the Catholic church. If you were outside it, you were lost, they said. Protestant reformer John Calvin located the line in the mind of God. The destiny of men and women was already decided before they were born through their predestination by the eternal will of the Creator. Martin Luther, on the other hand, placed the line within the realm of human volition, aided by divine grace. Salvation was the gift of God granted in response to the individual's act of faith in the Lord Jesus Christ.

Common to all of them, however, was the belief that outside Christendom lay only the inevitability of damnation. Heathendom, as it was called, was considered a legitimate target for both Christian contempt and evangelistic pity. The church understood its task as taking the Christian faith to non-Christians and offering them the opportunity to come into the church and be saved.

Contemporary theology, however, is disposed to make more careful distinctions about the world beyond the boundaries of the church. The great religions of the world may not be lumped together with other more ephemeral and less substantial beliefs. EST and Islam are not equivalents in the history of human spirituality. Evangelism in the modern context, therefore, requires a more sensitive and discriminating (in the best sense of the word) approach to the task of witnessing to Christ's saving love and forgiveness. It is still the purpose of the church to make Christ known throughout the earth by works of devotion and service, to share the *evangel* of Jesus Christ with all mankind. A sensitive evangelism, however, is diaconal rather than imperial in method, designed for service not conquest. It aims to show forth the Lord Jesus in acts of witness and faith rather than to "win souls" who are deemed otherwise to be lost.

The Prayer Book arose out of an era which interpreted the Great Commission of Jesus as a mandate for conquest. The late mediaeval church possessed great knowledge of the world and its cultures, but understood them all to be inferior to the native culture of Europe, and regarded all religions other than Christianity as mired in ignorance and error. When the Church of England began, it took over this outlook quite naturally and uncritically, and applied it to the expansionism which marked the goals of the powerful British Empire. An imperial theology characterized the Anglican approach to other religious traditions, which is articulated shamelessly in the traditional rites. Thus, the collect for Good Friday in the 1662 Prayer Book reads:

Have mercy upon all Jews, Turks, Infidels and Hereticks, and take from them all ignorance, hardness of heart, and contempt of thy Word; and so fetch them home, blessed Lord, to thy flock,

188 Rites for a New Age

that they may be saved among the remnant of the true Israelites, and be made one fold under one Shepherd.

There is revealed in this prayer a tendency to lump together all beliefs other than the Christian faith and to treat them all negatively without any attempt to make careful theological distinctions between them. Judaism, Islam, and heresies originating within the church itself are all alike viewed as a contempt of God's word — a breathtaking collection of different viewpoints encompassed within one phrase. Developed and sophisticated religious systems of thought are not distinguished from animistic or merely superstitious cults, but simply dismissed together as ignorance and hardness of heart. The Jewish faith, in particular, received harsh treatment from the early Anglican liturgists. Our church, along with others, has an historic tradition of rejection of Jewish belief which goes beyond mere theological disagreement, but approaches anti-Semitism. Thus, for example, the prayer for the conversion of the Jews in the 1662 edition:

Let us pray for the faithless Jews: that our God and Lord would take away the veil from their hearts; that they also may acknowledge Jesus Christ, our Lord.

And again,

Almighty God, who deniest not thy mercy even unto the faithless Jews; graciously hear our prayers, which we offer for the blindness of this people, that they, acknowledging the light of thy truth, may be delivered from their darkness.

Christians born into a post-Holocaust age now know the disastrous and evil consequences of this ancient mentality. The smoke from the ovens of Auschwitz has carried this prayer, and the attitude behind it, to heaven where, no doubt, we shall one day have to answer for it before the God of Abraham, Isaac, and Jacob — who is also the God of our Lord Jesus Christ. The 1962 revisions to the Canadian Prayer Book took out some of the more virulent anti-Semitic phrases, and a letter to the clergy from Archbishop Ted Scott in the 1982 asked that parishes no longer use the traditional Reproaches on Good Friday, which constitute a perpetuation of hardline attitudes.

The *Book of Alternative Services* marks a radical departure from this insupportable theology of malice. In a moving and eloquent devotion for Good Friday, the new rite replaces the anti-Semitic tone of the Reproaches with a meditation on the cross of Jesus. In it is contained this penitential dialogue:

> I grafted you into the tree of my chosen Israel,
> and you turned on them with persecution
> and mass murder.
> I made you joint heirs with them of my covenants,
> but you made them scapegoats for your own guilt.
>> Holy God, holy and mighty,
>> holy and immortal one, have mercy upon us.
>
> (*BAS* p.316)

In Anglican liturgical parlance, this is as close as one can get to an official apology to the Jews. Furthermore, there are no prayers for their conversion to the Christian faith and no intimations that to be Jewish is to be "faithless" or to be in ignorance or hardness of heart and so on. In fact, two of the six eucharistic prayers go out of their way to reject the implication that the suffering and death of Christ is an excuse to revile or hate the Jews:

> On the night he freely gave himself to death. . . .
> (eucharistic prayer 1 p.194)

> On the night he was handed over
> to suffering and death,
> a death he freely accepted. . . . .
> (eucharistic prayer 3 p.199)

This slight but very significant addition to the eucharistic rite is intended to emphasize the nature of our Lord's passion as self-offering, freely chosen by him and the Father as the means of human redemption. The voluntary and intentional nature of Christ's sacrifice therefore forbids Christians from looking upon the Jews as Christ killers, and requires of us a much greater understanding of the gospel and of our own scriptures than we have hitherto shown. The silence of the new rites on the matter of various evangelistic attempts to convert Jews to Christianity is a testimony to the new sensitivity of Anglicans in the aftermath of this century's racial Holocaust. It also indicates a shift in theological perspective which has implications for our relationship with other great religious traditions of the world as well.

Where the Prayer Book expressed a theology of exclusion of other faiths, the *Book of Alternative Services* expresses the rather more careful hope that the world may believe, that all people may come into God's kingdom and know God's salvation. Many petitions and intercessions express the plea that the kingdom of God may come upon all the earth, and that the whole human family may experience the promised fullness of life. Take, for example, the collect for the ninth Sunday after Epiphany (proper 9):

Lord God of the nations,
you have revealed your will to all people
and promised us your saving help.
May we hear and do what you command,
that the darkness may be overcome
by the power of your light.
(*BAS* p.359)

The rites do not attempt to dictate to God how the promised salvation shall come about. They express no particular program of political change, nor claim that the kingdom of God is the same thing as the worldwide dominion of the church. In fact, the language of the rites is as eloquent in what it does not say as in what it does. The skilful eye will detect a theology of salvation which places God at the centre of the task of human redemption, and not the church. The mission of the church is to place itself at the disposal of God so that its members may become instruments of God's will for human life. It is a nuance which allows a place for men and women of other traditions to be included in God's design, not necessarily by joining the church. This is not a low doctrine of the church but a high doctrine of God. It indicates a tension one finds throughout the *Book of Alternative Services* between evangelism and inter-faith dialogue. On the one hand, the church's task is to fulfil the Great Commission, but on the other hand modern Christians realize that they are not the sole religious occupants of the planet, and that a new sensitivity is required to members of other religious traditions. This tension is a creative one, no attempt being made in the book to resolve it, and is the context in which the church today must worship.

This tension does not in any way reduce the centrality of Christ in the mystery of God's redemption, however. The *Book of Alternative Services* expresses the historic Christian commitment to Jesus Christ as Saviour of the world, through whom people everywhere may come into the riches of God's kingdom. The collect for the Naming of Jesus (January 1) reads as follows:

Eternal Father,
we give thanks for your incarnate Son,
whose name is our salvation.
Plant in every heart, we pray,
the love of him who is the Saviour of the world,
our Lord Jesus Christ.
(*BAS* p.277)

The universal character of the atonement wrought by God through the death and resurrection of Christ is not thereby diminished, but the claim is not made that all people everywhere must come into the church in order to be saved. The new rites are careful to pray for the love of Christ to be planted in every heart, a possibility which is in principle open to members of other religious traditions. This does not relativize the centrality of Christ, nor does it minimize the dignity of other world religions. The way to the kingdom is through Christ and because of Christ. The new rites maintain simply that all who are baptized into Christ and follow him in faith are made heirs of the promises of God revealed in the scriptures. It does not make the claim that those who are not, do not. The actual list of who is or is not saved is known to God alone and cannot be within the church's power to determine. Salvation, in other words, is a gift of God, not of the church.

To conclude, the great theologian Thomas Aquinas wrote: "Peace is not the absence of tension, but the presence of justice." Mission and evangelism might be described as the effort to build a just peace, both within the individual heart and within the human community. Neither can be achieved at the expense of the other. There is a false polarization among Christians today between those who interpret the gospel as a call to social change (mission) and those who interpret it as a call to interior conversion (evangelism). While individual members of the church often have gifts in one or other of these directions, the wholeness of the gospel requires that both of them be held together. This is attempted in a commendable way by the *Book of Alternative Services*. No claim is being made, of course, that a book of rites by itself can achieve conversion, or a world of justice and peace. Only God, working in us, can do that. But the people of God at worship can be opened to this activity of God, and this we must be if humanity and the gospel are to survive the many threats of extinction in post-Christendom.

Questions for Discussion

1. Which of these statements about mission do you support? Mission is:
   - going to a foreign country
   - converting other people to our way of life
   - raising money to send missionaries overseas
   - preaching the gospel to the heathen
   - liberating the oppressed
   - supporting people to help themselves
   - standing up for the poor
   - witnessing to Christ wherever we are.

   Discuss your answers and give reasons.

2. What would be an authentic evangelism for the church today?
3. What should be the Christian approach to other religions of the world?
4. What do you understand by Jesus' blessing upon peace-makers, as distinct from peace-lovers?

8. Play

Almighty and everliving God,
increase in us your gift of faith,
that forsaking what lies behind
and reaching out to what is before,
we may run the way of your commandments
and win the crown of everlasting joy.
(Collect for proper 29: *BAS* p.387)

One of the many things we have learned from the social sciences is the importance of play. The games people play have a formative effect on their imagination and on their development. Children are shaped by their games to form particular attitudes and behaviours, which they carry with them into adult life (some of which they have to unlearn: see Carol Gilligan, *In a Different Voice*, quoted in chapter four). Adults are shaped by a large and powerful entertainment industry to form certain habits of spending, or even of thinking. Television, sports, even conventional jokes and humour, have a formative influence on adult opinion and actions. They are the symbols through which our culture perpetuates itself. Children's toys and games are a means by which society shapes their minds and educates them into their roles as future citizens and decision makers. Play, therefore, is not a trivial thing. We become what we play. We are shaped and formed by the many social and cultural forms of enjoyment into persons who act out in real life what we only imagine or dream about in our moments of entertainment. The unreal world which is symbolized in play is made actual and real through our unique human capacity to turn these dreams into reality.

Liturgy is also a kind of play. It is a way of playing before God, a divine play. By this I don't mean that liturgy is just a game with no real meaning. On the contrary, it is a symbolic drama which has a crucial meaning. Liturgy shapes and forms us for eternal life. It builds up in us a complex range of conscious and unconscious attitudes and behaviours just as surely as Monday night football (though, of course, in quite a different direction). It creates in our minds an imaginary world called the kingdom of God, and allows us to live vicariously in it for an hour or so, and then bids us go out into the actual world and make the kingdom world real within it. The worship of the church is a fragile earthen vessel containing the symbols and stories of our faith which, when acted out, become our personal symbols and stories, transforming our minds and behaviour and shaping us to conform with the images they represent.

There have been many books and articles in the last twenty years characterizing worship as a form of clowning before God, a divine foolishness. For Anglicans who are overly serious about worship and cling to a ponderous solemnity in the belief that this alone is reverence, this is a startling thought. But worship is indeed a symbol-language. All its elements have a dramatic quality. We stand, we sit, we kneel — we use our bodies to symbolize penitence or praise. We sing songs and walk about in processions. We consume bread and wine with awe and wonder, and our leaders dress up in colourful costumes. We light candles and sometimes wave fragrant smoke through the rooms where we meet. Our buildings are dressed like theatre sets, with coloured glass telling stories from the past, the structures themselves pointing to the east and mostly shaped like a cross. The more adventurous souls among us have taken to things like liturgical dance, gospel dramatizations, lively and joyful music, and innovative forms of preaching and teaching (though these have sometimes transgressed the limits of taste). Others merely observe their simple devotions day in and day out with unfailing persistence and without overt display. But all are involved in play before God, the Holy One who comes to meet us in symbol and song, the Lord who can, at any moment, break open the time and space of liturgy and transport us into a quite different dimension, to the very centre of the divine life itself.

The rites of the church, therefore, are of more than merely theological or historical significance. They shape and form us. They change our outlook and perceptions, and create new visions and dreams for us to make into reality, at least in our hearts. They influence profoundly the nature of our relationship with God.

Liturgy is work. It is a form of action in which we open ourselves to the possibility of being remade and reformed into a new creation. The content and style of the rites is therefore crucial to our identity and to an understanding of what we have become and are becoming. A change in the rites means a change in our identity, a change in our spirituality, and that is why liturgical renewal is so painful. It means we are called to become a people other than we presently are, to enter into new relationships with the God who comes to meet us, and few of us undertake that task gladly.

For 400 years the Prayer Book has shaped our corporate and individual lives. It has nurtured and sustained us through the last four centuries of Christendom. It has shaped us into a liturgical community. That familiar little red book has provided a basis for daily prayer and for public devotion. It has taught us to balance the various elements of western Christianity, particularly the different insights of the Protestant and Catholic traditions, into a creative and imaginative whole. It has resisted narrow and extremist schools of thought and interpretation, and encouraged in us a spirit of moderation and tolerance for the whole people of God. It has established in our church the practice of worshipping in the common tongue, and has made available to the church the liturgical resources necessary for growth in faith and ministry. But it is a part, not the sum, of our living tradition.

The Prayer Book is a book of its time. It reflects the political, cultural, and ecclesiastical norms of a century long gone. It was written for a church with a particular reality, but one which has now been transformed into a different reality by circumstances beyond our comprehension. It was designed to equip the faithful for life in a context where Christianity was the religion of all the people, and where the church was a powerful voice in the affairs of state. It was written for a world where one did not have to take seriously the other religious paths by which people have come to know God, nor where there was any reason to question the supremacy of men in the ordering of society. And it was designed to form in men and women a penitential spirituality, a way of approach to God which focused on the sinfulness of the human situation and the priority of individual salvation.

But the world has changed, and with it have changed many of our perspectives and priorities. We are being formed now by new rites for a new age. The *Book of Alternative Services* will shape us for the present as well as the future, for a time in which, as far as we can see, we will find ourselves a minority in a religiously pluralistic environment. It is an imperative of the Prayer Book itself that it should give rise to adaptation and amendment as the context of the church evolves. And there is much that remains constant and stable. We have retained our sense of balance and moderation, and we are growing stronger in our sense of being a liturgical, and particularly a eucharistic, community. But there is also much that is new for post-Christendom Christians, and much that is exciting.

We are being shaped by the new rites into a people moving outward in faith, conscious again of the power of the Spirit. We are being moulded into new relationships with one another, relationships of mutuality and equality, of caring and mutual support, and called to build new relationships within society of justice and peace. Our worship today is attempting to help us discover our individual gifts, to celebrate them, to contribute them to the work of Christ in the world and in the church, and to see ourselves as engaged always and everywhere in ministry as Christ's ambassadors. That ministry is presented to us as a servant ministry, not a campaign of conquest. We are being shaped into persons who will make Christ known through diaconal love, and in our ability to receive as well as to give. We are being called to renounce cultural domination and technological superiority, and to share the resources of the earth in a spirit of reverence for all created life.

In order to survive as marginal people in a biblically illiterate age the serious preparation of new members for incorporation into the church is now being required of us. Those coming to Christ as enquirers or as converts are to be welcomed more openly and instructed more intentionally. The baptism of new Christians is a sacramental activity involving the whole community, and we should now start to see fewer baptized unbelievers populating the country as the practice of social baptisms withers away. However, those who are received into the community of faith have every right to expect that they will be supported by the religious community through the joys and sorrows of their life, and will be challenged to grow in faith and loving service to those who do not yet know Christ. The *Book of Alternative Services* envisages the emergence of a community that will struggle to do all this.

It assumes also that the society in which we are to struggle is a society in need of the gospel of life. Threatened as we are on every side by the forces of death, by the dreadful spectre of nuclear winter, consumerism, unemployment, and the massive violations of human dignity, the new rites make a brave attempt to lift up before us the risen Christ and to point us toward the God who brings life out of death in all ages and circumstances. They centre contemporary Christian spirituality in Easter and Pentecost, calling us to cross a new frontier of hope and optimism even in the face of all the obvious dangers of the modern situation. They bid us rise and stand in the presence of God, not because we are worthy, but because Christ has made us worthy through his love and redemptive sacrifice. They ask us to re-know ourselves as a royal priesthood, consecrated for service by the death and resurrection of our Lord, and invited to share in the heavenly feast in the life everlasting.

They assume also that the church itself is no longer the uniform and liturgically unvarying institution it once was. They contain an implicit statement that the modern church in a vast and regionally varied country like ours has differing liturgical needs and opportunities in different times and places. The complexity of the new book is evidence of a new sensitivity in the church to its own reality, an effort not to confuse but to unify the diversity of our life and worship. It recognizes that flexibility and pluralism can be made into strengths, not just regarded as weaknesses, and it attempts to create a constant and regular pattern of liturgy within which are offered a multiplicity of variations. Only time and continuous usage of the book will tell whether the enterprise has been well-or ill-conceived (and that time is not now), but it is certainly no mistake to have attempted it, and the effort cannot be rejected simply on account of the grandeur of its scale.

Nor should it be rejected simply on account of the modernity of its style. Language is, as I have argued, the vehicle of meaning, and almost all our meanings have changed since Cranmer wrote his gorgeous prose. Nothing can compare with the beauty and elegance of Tudor English, and let it be confessed that the *Book of Alternative Services* is less than its parent in linguistic wealth. But the issue here is not language but liturgy, not sound but content. One does not go to church to worship a book but to praise and glorify the living God. That God is one who has entered history and speaks through the experience and language of everyday culture. Our access to this transcendent Lord is not confined to particular linguistic forms, nor to particular symbols or buildings. The God who has spoken in our history nevertheless exists beyond all human imagination and words, and certainly exists beyond the images and descriptions of our little Prayer Book (and, no less of course, our little *Book of Alterative Services*). Words and style are not the issue in this evolution of our rites. The issue is whether we will accept the challenge of a new age, and strive for new forms and structures to meet it.

New wine, as our Lord remarked, cannot be put into old wineskins. The old, beloved, and well-proven vessel will not contain a reality to which it is not suited. This does not deny its continuing validity. The Prayer Book is still with us, and will continue to be with us for the lifetime of anyone reading this book. It represents our heritage, our past, our memory, and the record of who we once were and from whence we have come. It reminds us of our historic identity, and still, and always will, points the soul to heaven, and remains a vehicle for devout absorption into God. There is no secret plan to abandon it or to replace it with the new book (the *Book of Alternative Services* is just that, and it should not be called a new Prayer Book — see the introduction on p.8). But nevertheless it belongs to the age of Christendom and will be of greatest value only to those who wish to remain there, forever dwelling in the imagined Golden Age.

For the rest of our lifetime we will belong to a church which has two liturgical traditions existing simultaneously one with the other, side by side. Each has its value, and each will contribute to the other, enriching the worship of the church and the spirituality of their devout users. If the day should come when what is old is finally and irrevocably left behind, when the church embraces with hope and courage a new way and a new vision, it will not be because of some conspiracy by the hierarchy to rob the members of their birthright, but because the Spirit will make it inevitable. We belong to a God who calls us out of comfortable familiarity and into an unknown future. We are members of a body whose head is one who promised to lead us into all truth, a truth which would set us free. We have been baptized with an unpredictable Spirit. If these things can be finally and deeply grasped, then the *Book of Alternative Services* will have been as much a service to the post-Christendom church as its predecessor was to our forebears.

Come, Holy Spirit, wisdom and truth: strengthen us in the risk of faith.
Come, Holy Spirit, come.
(*BAS* p.123)